BASIC BUSINESS MATH:

A Life-Skills Approach
Revised

Richard P. Truchon

A FIFTY-MINUTE™ SERIES BOOK

CRISP PUBLICATIONS, INC.
Menlo Park, California

BASIC BUSINESS MATH:
A Life-Skills Approach
Revised

Richard P. Truchon

CREDITS
Editor: **Tony Hicks**
Production: **Leslie Power**
Typesetting: **ExecuStaff**
Cover Design: **Carol Harris**

Printed in the United States of America

Distribution to the U.S. Trade:

National Book Network, Inc.
4720 Boston Way
Lanham, MD 20706
1-800-462-6420

Language of Algebra, glossary, pages 141–142
Reprinted with permission from *Essential Mathematics with Applications,* Trivieri
McGraw-Hill, Inc., 1988
Mathematics Study Skills, pages 1–5
Adapted from *Study Skills Strategies,* Uelaine Lengefeld
Crisp Publications, 1988

Library of Congress Catalog Card Number 97-65867
Truchon, Richard P.
Basic Business Math
ISBN 1-56052-448-0

This book is printed on recyclable paper with soy ink.

10 9 8 7 6 5 4 3 2 1

PREFACE

There is an emerging knowledge economy that is impacting our country's global leadership. Countries such as Japan and West Germany have a higher mathematics and science proficiency than the United States. On a more personal level, each of us must become more numerate if we wish to succeed in the ever-changing technological environment. Knowledge permeates every aspect of our lives, because our knowledge translates into highly skilled jobs, higher wages, and a better quality of life.

This book was written to help the reader improve his or her basic mathematics skills using a self-study approach. The book follows this structure: the introduction to each concept is followed by examples and exercises. In doing the exercises, it is strongly recommended that the reader use a calculator. Calculators are commonly used throughout the business world.

The best way to learn mathematics is to solve problems! This book will enable you to improve your basic skills in a friendly, practical way. To paraphrase an ancient Chinese proverb: When I hear mathematics, I think about it; when I see mathematics, I remember it; when I do mathematics, I understand it.

This text uses mathematical knowledge and skills to solve problems that commonly occur in business and at home. We all encounter such life-skill problems as working with percentage, ratio, and proportion; paying sales tax; borrowing or investing money; being paid a commission; purchasing discounted products on sale; using credit cards; and so on. As educated people, we need to understand the mathematics used in these situations. We can't always rely on someone else to do our thinking for us.

When you have mastered the information in this text, you will be better prepared to use mathematics in business.

New features to this edition include the following:

- The use of metrics in some of the exercise problems and illustrations
- A section on compound interest calculation
- An expansion of Part IV (Graphs and Statistics) to include the basic statistics of mean, median, mode, range, and standard deviation
- New illustrations and exercise problems
- Use of [a b/c] key—found on many scientific calculators

ABOUT THE AUTHOR

Richard P. Truchon is a professor at New Hampshire Community Technical College in Manchester and an adjunct professor at NECC in Havershill, Massachusetts. He is a member of Phi Kappa Phi, The Honor Society, The Associates of Teachers of Mathematics in New England, and the Massachusetts Teachers Association. He is listed in *Who's Who in American Education,* 4th Edition, 1995; *The Dictionary of International Biography,* 24th Edition, 1995; and *Who's Who Among America's Teachers,* 3rd Edition, 1994.

When he is not teaching Mr. Truchon enjoys the following hobbies: gardening, hiking, cross-country skiing, mountain climbing, reading, and listening to classical music.

ABOUT THE SERIES

With over 200 titles in print, the acclaimed Crisp 50-Minute™ series presents self-paced learning at its easiest and best. These comprehensive self-study books for business or personal use are filled with exercises, activities, assessments, and case studies that capture your interest and increase your understanding.

Other Crisp products, based on the 50-Minute books, are available in a variety of learning style formats for both individual and group study, including audio, video, CD-ROM, and computer-based training.

CONTENTS

CONTENTS (continued)

ACKNOWLEDGMENTS

I thank my colleagues at New Hampshire Community Technical College, Professors Samuel Robinson and Eugene Rice, for their suggestions and reviews of the manuscript. Thanks are also extended by my students who were assigned many of the exercises, for this gave me the stimulus to continue writing.

Thanks to my faculty secretary, Joanne Page, for quickly and competently word processing the text revision I gave her on a daily basis. I am most appreciative of the contributions made by Leslie Power, Production Editor at Crisp.

Finally, I wish to thank my wife, Lorraine, for her continued support, patience, and faith during the writing of this book.

This book is dedicated to my wife
Lorraine

P A R T

I

Basics

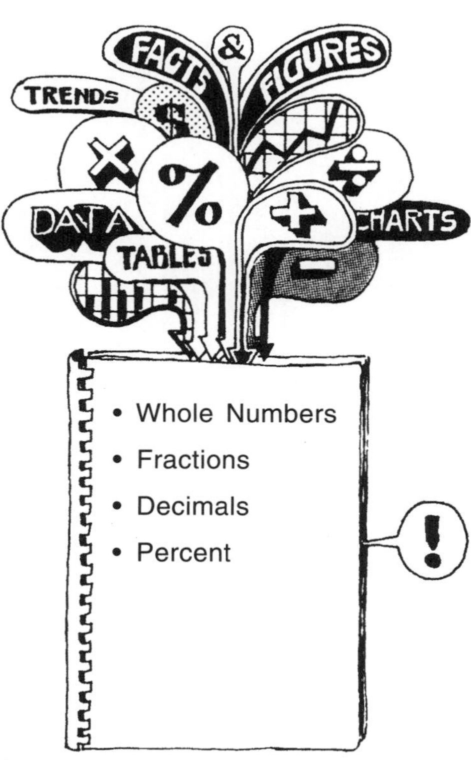
FACTS
&
FIGURES
TRENDS
%
DATA
TABLES
CHARTS
• Whole Numbers
• Fractions
• Decimals
• Percent
!

MATHEMATICS STUDY SKILLS

Mathematics requires special study skill techniques. This brief section will provide a few tips and ideas that should make your math study skills more effective.

Because math can be confusing, it will sometimes be necessary to ask for special help. If you become confused or lost, seek the assistance of a tutor. Mathematics often builds on a set of rules, and if basic principles are not understood, the likelihood is that you will stay lost.

TIPS

TIP 1 Copy all the theorems, principles, and definitions *exactly*. Do not paraphrase or condense anything that is written on the board. *Also* be sure to copy the instuctor's explanation. Draw arrows to the instructor's explanation for each step of the problem.

TIP 2 Rewrite math notes each day in ink for clarity and permanence. *Neatness* is especially important because of the need for accuracy.

TIP 3 *Rework model problems* over and over until you can do them without stopping. This is the crucial step that most students overlook. Instead of figuring out what is being taught in the model problem, they jump right into doing homework and end up reworking problems several times.

TIP 4 Plan to work *at least two hours* on math homework for every hour of class time. Since you may need to spend ten to twelve hours working on math class assignments, set your priorities carefully and take a lighter academic load if possible.

TIP 5 Learn the five Rs of math shown on the next page.

THE FIVE Rs OF MATH

R_1 RECOPY YOUR NOTES

R_2 REWORK THE MODEL

R_3 RECITE OUT LOUD

R_4 RECHECK YOUR WORK

R_5 TEST YOUR ANSWERS FOR REASONABLENESS

PLAN OF ATTACK

To help you get an overview of the best math study skills, read the following five Rs for Math. Write recall cues to help you remember R_1, R_2, R_3, R_4, and R_5.

THE 5 Rs OF MATH

RECALL CUES

______

______ R_1

______

RECOPY your notes in pen. Color-code definitions, rules, and problem areas. Neatness and legibility are your first step toward becoming a better math student.

How do you rate your math notes?

- ❑ Organized and clear
- ❑ Messy
- ❑ Disorganized but neat

______

______ R_2

______

REWORK the model or example over and over until you can do it without hestitation.

Have you ever taken this step before beginning the exercises?

❑ YES ❑ NO

If not, try it and see if it makes a difference.

______

______ R_3

______

RECITE. Oral recitation is one more technique for improving your mathematical skills. Practice this step with a study partner or friend. Force each other to explain out loud each step of the process. If you are studying alone, you can still express your thinking aloud.

Have you ever used this oral recitation technique when you were studying math?

❑ YES ❑ NO

(Problem solving out loud is not a sign of senility but the mark of a critical thinker.)

PLAN OF ATTACK (continued)

RECHECK your computations. Also recheck your thinking process. This is even more important when you move from one step of a problem to the next, or from one concept to a new one.

> **"MINDCHATTER"***
>
> When the internal thinking of professionals was questioned and recorded by Dr. Arthur Whimbey and Dr. Jack Lochhead, a typical dialogue was similar to the following:
>
> 1. "Let me read the question again to be sure what's being asked. I'll circle or underline the question."
> 2. "Okay. I see, but I'll read it again to be sure."
> 3. "Slow down. Don't rush."
> 4. "What is given? What is known?"
> 5. "How can I diagram, make a chart, or draw a visual to help me?"
>
> In all cases, lawyers, doctors, engineers, and other professionals were painstakingly careful to reread phrases and double-check their work.

Test for **REASONABLENESS.** Plug your answer into the problem to see if it makes sense. This final check could save you time and embarrassment later.

> Asking questions about how reasonable an answer is will make critical thinking a habit and problem solving less ominous.

* Adapted from Arthur Whimbey and Jack Lochhead, *Problem Solving and Comprehension*, 4th ed. (Lawrence Erlbaum Associates, 1986).

1.0 WHOLE NUMBERS

Most of us are familiar with two languages: a qualitative language (such as English or French) and a quantitative language (mathematics). In our qualitative language we use symbols (words) to represent concepts; for example, the word *dog* represents a dog. Similarly, in our quantitative language we use symbols (numbers) to represent number concepts; for example, *391* represents the number three hundred ninety-one. The arrangement of the symbols is important. The meaning of the concept will change if we write *god* instead of *dog*, or *193* in place of *391*. The letters of the alphabet are our written qualitative symbols; the digits of our number system are our quantitative symbols. In this text we will limit our discussion to the decimal or base-ten number system.

As children we learned about mathematics by counting with the *natural numbers:* 1, 2, 3, 4, 5, 6, 7, 8, 9. Later the number zero was introduced to give us a set of numbers known as the *whole numbers.* Each digit in a whole number has a place value. Moving from right to left increases the place value by a multiple of ten.

Example 1. Indicate the place values of the number 391.

3	9	1
Hundreds	Tens	Ones

"391" thus represents

$$\begin{aligned} 3 \times 100 &= 300 \\ 9 \times 10 &= 90 \\ 1 \times 1 &= \underline{1} \\ & 391 \end{aligned}$$

or

$$300 + 90 + 1 = 391$$

This number is read as "three hundred ninety-one."

Note: The word *and* is not used in reading whole numbers. We need to know how to write numbers as words and conversely whenever we write checks.

1.0 WHOLE NUMBERS (continued)

Example 2. What number does "42,113,786" represent?

4 2, 1 1 3, 7 8 6 represents

4 ×	10,000,000	=	40,000,000
2 ×	1,000,000	=	2,000,000
1 ×	100,000	=	100,000
1 ×	10,000	=	10,000
3 ×	1,000	=	3,000
7 ×	100	=	700
8 ×	10	=	80
6 ×	1	=	6
			42,113,786

40,000,000 + 2,000,000 + 100,000 + 10,000 + 3,000 + 700 + 80 + 6 = 42,113,786

This number is read as "forty-two million, one hundred thirteen thousand, seven hundred eighty-six."

1.1 Rounding Off Whole Numbers

When we say that a corporation's annual profit is $240,000, we are using an approximation. It may be that the actual profit is $239,781, but it is easier to use the number $240,000. The number has been *rounded off* to the nearest ten thousand. We rounded the number to $240,000 rather than $230,000 because $239,781 is closer to $240,000 than to $230,000. Here are some other examples of rounding off: 47 rounded to the nearest ten is 50; and 3,741 rounded to the nearest hundred is 3,700.

The procedure for rounding off whole numbers is:

1. Underline the digit in the place you are rounding to.
2. Look at the digit immediately to the right of the underlined digit. If the digit immediately to the right is greater than or equal to 5, add 1 to the underlined digit. If the digit immediately to the right is less than 5, don't change the underlined digit.
3. Replace all digits to the right of the underlined digit with zeros.

Example 1. Round 357 to the nearest hundred.

STEP 1 Underline the hundreds digit: 357

STEP 2 Look at the digit immediately to the right of the underlined digit. That digit is 5, so we increase 3 by 1: 457

STEP 3 Replace all digits to the right of the underlined digit with zeros: 400.

Example 2. Round 350 to the nearest hundred.

$350 \approx 400$

This is read as "three hundred fifty is approximately equal to four hundred."

Example 3. Round 341 to the nearest hundred.

$341 \approx 300$

We will return to the concept of rounding off when we discuss decimals.

1.0 WHOLE NUMBERS (continued)

EXERCISE 1.1

1. Indicate the place value of each digit in the number 4,391.

2. Indicate the place value of the digit 7 in the number 8,473.

3. Write eleven thousand, three hundred sixty-two in figures.

4. Write seven million, four hundred three in figures.

5. Write 345,678 in words.

6. Write 19,191 in words.

7. Indicate the place value of each digit in the number 5,012.

8. Name the place value of 7 in the number 173,245.

9. Write one hundred seventeen thousand, three hundred forty-seven in figures.

10. Write 1,234 in words.

11. Write 403,057 in words.

12. Round 3,948 to the nearest ten.

13. Round 3,948 to the nearest hundred.

14. Round 169,750 to the nearest hundred thousand.

15. Round 7,500 to the nearest thousand.

1.2 Addition of Whole Numbers

The most frequently used operation is addition. The numbers being added are called *addends* and the result of the operation is called the *sum*.

Example 1. Add 2 + 11 + 3.

2 + 11 + 3 = 16
addends sum

Example 2. Add 341 + 24 + 19.

```
  341
   24   addends
+  19
  ---
  384   sum
```

Since most businesses use computers today, you will find both the vertical and horizontal forms of addition when you use an electronic spreadsheet or other software.

Example 3. Use a calculator to add 68 + 47 + 2,051. The calculator sequence is:

[68] [+] [47] [+] [2051] [=] *2,166*

1.0 WHOLE NUMBERS (continued)

EXERCISE 1.2

1. Add: 72
33
+ 15

2. Add: 407
939
241
+ 102

3. Add: 43 + 21 + 67.

4. The Pennyroyal Herb Farm had the following expenses during the month of June.

Advertising	$ 217	Supplies	$54
Rent	$ 934	Electricity	$98
Salaries	$3,478	Miscellaneous	$39

What were the total expenses for the month?

5. The Shop and Save supermarket has been monitoring the sales of three different brands of cornflakes on a daily basis.

(a) Use the spreadsheet below to determine the sales of all three brands each day.
(b) Also determine the total sales of each brand for the week.
(c) What were the total sales of all brands for the week?

	MON	TUES	WED	THURS	FRI	SAT	TOTAL
Brand K	4	10	7	11	15	5	
Brand P	15	6	14	8	22	11	
Brand G	7	13	9	9	10	9	

6. Add: 1,307
422
196
18
+ 3,002

7. Add: 1,492 + 203 + 1,938 + 64 + 373.

8. Charles had a balance of $713 in his checking account. He made the following deposits: $35, $118, $59, and $142. What is his new balance?

9. The attendance at a weekend rock concert was 23,450 on Saturday afternoon, 39,975 on Saturday evening and 32,288 on Sunday evening. What was the total attendance for the three performances?

10. Your biweekly paycheck shows the following deductions: FICA, $76; federal income tax, $85; retirement fund, $51; health insurance, $7; union dues, $3. What is the total amount of your deductions?

11. Use the spreadsheet below to determine (a) the commissions paid to all four salespersons each month, (b) the third-quarter commission for each salesperson, and (c) the total of commissions paid for the quarter.

Salesperson	July	August	September	Third-Quarter Commissions
Maria	$1,385	$ 1,300	$ 793	
Joe	$ 781	$ 3,750	$11,028	
Mohammed	$9,830	$10,123	$ 899	
Yoko	$1,010	$ 903	$10,452	

12. Brigitte ordered three items from a mail order company. The three items weighed 2 pounds, 7 ounces; 4 pounds, 8 ounces; and 3 pounds, 9 ounces. What was the total weight of the three items? (1 lb. = 16 oz.)

1.3 Subtraction of Whole Numbers

Subtraction is the operation of taking one number from another. The larger of the two numbers is called the *minuend.* The number being subtracted is called the *subtrahend.* The result of the subtraction is called the *difference.*

Example 1. Subtract 739 from 251.

```
  739  minuend
– 251  subtrahend
  488  difference
```

Example 2. Subtract $3 from $10.

$10	–	$3	=	$7
minuend		subtrahend		difference

Subtraction is related to addition. In a sense, subtraction is another way of looking at the operation of addition. For any two whole numbers M and S, if $M - S = D$, then $D + S = M$.

1.0 WHOLE NUMBERS (continued)

Example 3. Consider the subtraction in Example 1.

739 – 251 = 488

What number must be added to 251 to give a sum of 739? The answer is 488.

251 + 488 = 739

If we want to subtract a larger number from a smaller number, we need a knowledge of algebra. We have to use *negative numbers.* For example, if the balance in our checking account is $47 and we write a check for $53, we have a deficit of $6. The balance of our account is –$6. In this book we will concentrate on subtraction problems where M is bigger than S.

Example 4. Stephen has $597 in his checking account. If he writes a check for $103, how much money will be left in his account?

$597 – $103 = $494

Example 5. Use a calculator to subtract 234 from 1,007.

[1007] [–] [234] [=] *773*

Example 6. Allan telephoned Dick and spoke for 9 minutes and 25 seconds. Later that day, Allan called Dick again and spoke for 5 minutes and 33 seconds. How much longer was the first call than the second?

	9 min., 25 sec.
–	5 min., 33 sec.

We cannot subtract 33 seconds from 25 seconds, so we borrow 1 minute (60 seconds) from 9 minutes and convert 9 minutes, 25 seconds, to 8 minutes, 85 seconds.

Thus our problem becomes:

	8 min., 85 sec.
–	5 min., 33 sec.
	3 min., 52 sec.

The first call was 3 minutes and 52 seconds longer than the second.

EXERCISE 1.3

1. Subtract 309 from 1,103.

2. Subtract 46 from 7,801.

3. Mary's pet cat weighs 9 pounds 5 ounces and Jane's pet cat weighs 6 pounds, 7 ounces. How much more does Mary's cat weigh than Jane's? (1 lb. = 16 oz.)

4. Kate jogged for 37 minutes, 23 seconds, and Phil jogged for 23 minutes, and 43 seconds. (a) How much longer did Kate jog than Phil? (b) What was the combined jogging time for the two? (1 min. = 60 sec.)

5. $\begin{array}{r} 4{,}675 \\ -\underline{2{,}503} \end{array}$

6. Subtract 3,631 from 12,948.

7. 129,497 − 11,384 = ?

8. John has had $3,781 withheld from his wages this year. If he owes $2,973 in income taxes for the year, how much of a refund will he receive?

9. Find the difference between eleven hundred fifty-nine and three thousand, four hundred twelve.

10. Owner's equity is defined as the total assets minus the total liabilities. The August balance sheet for the Pennyroyal Tree Farm listed total assets at $247,934 and total liabilities at $213,529. Find the owner's equity.

11. Sam recently purchased a computer for $2,375 and wrote a check for $850 as a down payment. Find the amount that remains to be paid.

12. A real estate agent rented 23 apartments in April, 31 apartments in May, and 47 apartments in June. How many more apartments must be rented in July if the agent's four-month quota is 130 apartments?

1.0 WHOLE NUMBERS (continued)

1.4 Multiplication of Whole Numbers

Multiplication is repeated addition of the same numbers. For example, 7×3 means $7 + 7 + 7$.

$$7 \times 3 = 7 + 7 + 7 = 21$$

The number that is multiplied is called the *multiplicand.* The number we multiply by is called the *multiplier.* The result of the multiplication is called the *product.* The multiplicand and multiplier are also called *factors.*

When we multiply two numbers that have more than one digit, we multiply each digit of the multiplicand by each digit of the multiplier to obtain a partial product. The sum of all of the partial products is the product.

Example 1. Multiply 218 by 37.

218	multiplicand
× 37	multiplier
1,526	
+ 654	partial products
8,066	product

Example 2. Use a calculator to multiply 218 by 37.

[ON] [218] [×] [37] [=] *8066*

Example 3. If a gallon of paint costs $13 per gallon, how much would 27 gallons of paint cost?

$13 × 27 = $351

EXERCISE 1.4

1. Multiply 791 by 103.

2. What is the cost of 15 VCRs if 1 VCR costs $325?

3. A case of canned peas contains 24 cans. How many cans of peas would there be in 225 cases?

4. Michele bought seven concert tickets for $21 each and three more tickets for $15 each. What was her total bill?

5. If your monthly salary is $1,260 and you can expect a yearly raise of $126 per month, what would be your earnings over a three-year period?

6. A company orders 170 boxes of letterhead envelopes. If each box cost $23, find the total cost.

7. The division of community education at Calmina University charges tuition at a rate of $21 per credit. If a student has 15 credits during the fall semester, how much tuition will he pay?

8. Elizabeth is the buyer for a Boston department store. She purchased 19 cases of men's socks, containing 40 pairs of socks in each case. If the socks cost $3 a pair, what is the total cost of the purchase?

9. You drive for five hours at a speed of 55 miles per hour. How many miles did you travel?

10. Bob Hanson has a small apple orchard on his property. If each tree produces approximately three bushels of apples per season, how many bushels can he harvest from his orchard of 21 trees in one season?

11. It costs $31 a day, without mileage, to rent a car. How much does it cost to rent a car for 16 days, excluding mileage?

12. Skyway Airlines has eight flights from Boston to Hartford each day. How many passengers per day can Skyway Airlines transport from Boston to Hartford if each flight can carry 175 passengers?

1.0 WHOLE NUMBERS (continued)

1.5 Division of Whole Numbers

Division is finding how many times one number is contained in another. The number being divided is called the *dividend.* The number by which we are dividing is called the *divisor.* The result is called the *quotient.* If the divisor is not a multiple of the dividend, the remaining number is called a *remainder.*

Example 1. Divide 1,138 by 11.

```
                103      quotient
divisor     11)1,138     dividend
             -11
               38
              -33
                5        remainder
```

Just as multiplication can be thought of as repeated addition, so division can be thought of as repeated subtraction.

Example 2. Divide 35 by 5. Keep subtracting 5s from 35 until you're left with zero. The number of times that 5 is subtracted from 35 is the quotient. The quotient is 7 in this example.

	Number of subtractions		Number of subtractions
35		15	
− 5	1	− 5	5
30		10	
− 5	2	− 5	6
25		5	
− 5	3	− 5	7
20		0	
− 5	4		
15		0	

Multiplication and division are related operations. We can use multiplication to check our division. The divisor multiplied by the quotient will give the dividend, if there is a remainder of zero.

Example 3. Divide 35 by 5 and check the answer.

$$5\overline{)35}^{\,7}$$

Check: 7 × 5 = 35 The division is correct.

Note: The result of dividing by zero is undefined! You cannot divide by zero. Thus, 14 ÷ 0 has no answer.

Example 4. Use your calculator to try 14 by 0.

[14] [÷] [0] [=] *ERROR*

Occasionally students will forget that you can't divide by zero when they encounter 0 ÷ 0. Perhaps that error occurs because "any number divided by itself is one" is an often heard statement. The statement is incomplete, however; it should be, "any number *except zero* . . . "

Note that you can divide any number, except zero, into zero.

Example 5. Divide 0 by 7.

0 ÷ 7 = 0

Example 6. Use a calculator to divide 10,215 by 15.

[10215] [÷] [15] [=] *681*

Example 7. If a car can travel for 810 miles on 45 gallons of gasoline, how far can it travel on 1 gallon of gasoline?

$$45\overline{)810}^{\,18}$$

It can travel 18 miles on 1 gallon of gas.

The *average* of a set of addends is defined as the sum of the numbers divided by the number of numbers. To find the average of a set of numbers, add them, and then divide by the number of addends.

1.0 WHOLE NUMBERS (continued)

Example 8. Carla made the following deposits in her checking account: \$640, \$830, \$1,056, and \$700. What was Carla's average deposit?

STEP 1 Add the amounts of the deposits.

$$\begin{array}{r} \$640 \\ 830 \\ 1{,}056 \\ +\ \ 700 \\ \hline \$3{,}226 \end{array}$$

STEP 2 Divide the total amount deposited (\$3,226) by the number of deposits (4).

$$\begin{array}{r} \$806.50 \\ 4\overline{)3{,}226.00} \\ \underline{32} \\ 26 \\ \underline{24} \\ 20 \\ \underline{20} \\ 0 \end{array}$$

Example 9. The following daily temperatures were recorded during the first week in January: S, 13°; M, 32°; T, 27°; W, 14°; Th, 29°; F, 0°; S, 5°. Find the average temperature for the week, to the nearest 0.1° using a calculator.

[13] [+] [32] [+] [27] [+] [14] [+] [29] [+] [0]

[+] [5] [=] [÷] [7] [=] *17.1* The average temperature is 17.1°.

EXERCISE 1.5

1. Divide 960 by 16.

2. $0\overline{)0}$

3. On an English exam, six students' scores were 76, 83, 68, 90, 92, and 95. What was their average score?

4. A business ordered 800 personal computers (PCs) at a total cost of $760,000. Another order at the same price per PC came to $251,750. How many PCs were received on the second order?

5. (a) 624 ÷ 4 = ? (b) 63,525 ÷ 75 = ?

6. Find the quotient of forty-one thousand, one hundred forty divided by sixty-eight.

7. The total cost of producing 475 calculators was $12,825. What is the unit cost (that is, the cost of producing 1 calculator)?

8. Joey is expected to make an average of 7 sales calls per day. Last week she made 6 calls on Monday, 9 calls on Tuesday, 11 calls on Wednesday, 5 calls on Thursday, and 10 calls on Friday. What was Joey's average? Did she meet her quota?

9. How much do you earn per week if your annual salary is $40,716?

10. ABC company's monthly wages are: manager, $1,320; accountant, $1,175; 12 salespeople, $790 each; 2 bookkeepers, $630 each; custodian, $510. What is the average monthly wage of an ABC company employee?

11. On a math exam, two students scored 95, five students scored 87, three students scored 73, four students scored 63, and one student scored 40. What was the class average?

12. What is the gasoline mileage on a 489 mile trip if you used 12 gallons of gasoline?

2.0 FRACTIONS

Many business mathematics problems cannot be solved by using only whole numbers. Business people often need to compare two quantities. When one quantity is divided by a similar like quantity, such as

$$\frac{\text{Current assets}}{\text{Current liabilities}} = \$137{,}500$$

we have a *ratio,* also called a *fraction.* A fraction is one number, the *numerator,* divided by another number, the *denominator.*

Example 1. Write "three-fourths" as a fraction.

$$\frac{3}{4} \quad \begin{matrix}\text{numerator}\\ \text{denominator}\end{matrix}$$

The numerator is the number of equal parts being considered. The denominator is the number of equal parts that the whole has been divided into. The fraction $\frac{3}{4}$ can be represented as in Figure 2.1.

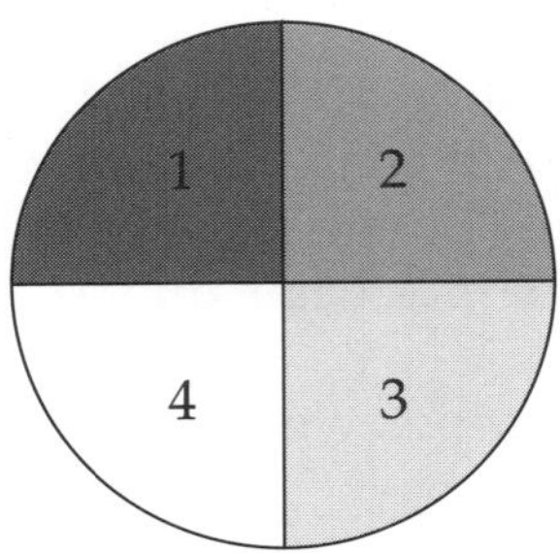

Figure 2.1 Three-fourths ($\frac{3}{4}$)

Recall that the only whole number that cannot be a denominator is zero. *Division by zero is impossible!* It is possible, however, to divide any whole number, except zero, into zero.

Example 2. What is the value of $\dfrac{7}{0}$?

The quantity $\frac{7}{0}$ does not exist. There's no number that can be multiplied by zero to give 7. Any number multiplied by zero gives a product of zero—never 7!

2.1 Proper and Improper Fractions

A *proper fraction* has a numerator that is less than its denominator, such as $\frac{3}{7}$. A proper fraction is smaller than 1. An *improper fraction* has a numerator that is greater than its denominator, such as $\frac{4}{3}$. An improper fraction is greater than 1.

Like fractions are fractions whose denominators are the same. For example, $\frac{1}{7}$, $\frac{3}{7}$, and $\frac{5}{7}$ are like fractions.

Unlike fractions are fractions whose denominators are different. For example, $\frac{1}{4}$, $\frac{2}{7}$, $\frac{5}{8}$, and $\frac{7}{11}$ are unlike fractions.

The fractions $\frac{5}{10}$, $\frac{6}{12}$, $\frac{7}{14}$, and $\frac{25}{50}$ could all be written as $\frac{1}{2}$. We say that $\frac{5}{10}$ is *reduced* or *simplified* to $\frac{1}{2}$, and that $\frac{5}{10}$ and $\frac{1}{2}$ are *equivalent fractions.* In any problem involving fractions it is usually helpful to reduce a fraction to its lowest terms before beginning your work. A fraction is reduced to its lowest terms if it can't be reduced any further, that is, if the only common factor of the numerator and denominator is 1.

Example 3. A *unity fraction,* or *unity ratio,* is any fraction that has a value of 1. Some examples of unity fractions are:

$$\frac{1\text{ lb.}}{16\text{ oz.}},\ \frac{60\text{ min.}}{1\text{ hr.}},\ \frac{1\text{ yd.}}{36\text{ in.}},\ \frac{1\text{ in.}}{60\text{ min.}}$$

Using unity fractions enables us to convert from one type of measure to a different equivalent.

$$60\text{ in.} = ?\text{ ft.}$$

$$(60\text{ in.})\underbrace{\left(\frac{1\text{ ft.}}{12\text{ in.}}\right)}_{\text{equals 1}} = \frac{60\text{ ft.}}{12},\text{ or 5 ft.}$$

Note: that the unit, inches, divides out and we are left with feet.

2.0 FRACTIONS (continued)

Example 4. Reduce $\frac{3}{12}$ to its lowest terms.

$$\frac{3}{12} = \frac{3 \times 1}{3 \times 4} = \frac{3}{3} \times \frac{1}{4} = 1 \times \frac{1}{4} = \frac{1}{4}$$

Example 5. Reduce $\frac{21}{56}$ to its lowest terms.

$$\frac{21}{56} = \frac{7 \times 3}{7 \times 8} = \frac{7}{7} \times \frac{3}{8} = 1 \times \frac{3}{8} = \frac{3}{8}$$

Here's a way to check whether two fractions are equivalent. Multiply the numerator of the first fraction by the denominator of the second fraction. Then multiply the numerator of the second fraction by the denominator of the first fraction. If the two products are equal, the fractions are equivalent.

Example 6. Are $\frac{3}{7}$ and $\frac{18}{42}$ equivalent?

$3 \times 42 = 126$
$7 \times 18 = 126$

Therefore, $\frac{3}{7}$ and $\frac{18}{42}$ are equivalent.

A *mixed number* consists of a whole number and a fraction, such as $2\frac{1}{3}$ read as "two and one-third." It is permissible to use the word *and* here. $2\frac{1}{3}$ means 2 and $\frac{1}{3}$, or 2 plus $\frac{1}{3}$.

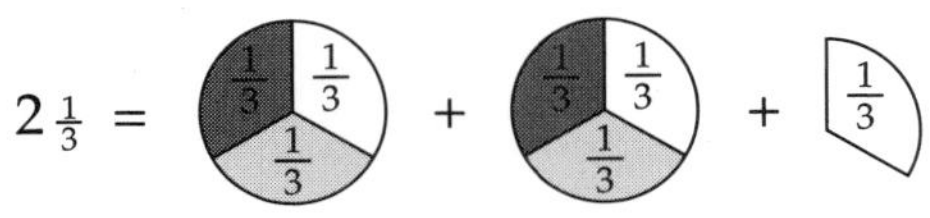

If we need to convert an improper fraction to a mixed number, we must divide the numerator by the denominator. The quotient is our whole number, and the remainder is the numerator of the fraction.

Example 7. Convert $\frac{5}{3}$ to a mixed number.

$$\begin{array}{rl} 1 & \text{whole number} \\ 3\overline{)5} & \\ \underline{3} & \\ 2 & \text{remainder} \end{array}$$

Therefore, $\frac{5}{3} = 1\frac{2}{3}$

Conversely, if we wish to convert a mixed number to an improper fraction, we multiply the whole number by the denominator and add the numerator. This gives the new numerator; the denominator remains the same.

Example 8. Convert $2\frac{5}{8}$ to an improper fraction.

$2 \times 8 + 5 = 16 + 5 = 21$

The denominator is 8. Therefore, $2\frac{5}{8} = \frac{21}{8}$.

Example 9. Reduce $\frac{222}{37}$ to its lowest terms.

$$\frac{222}{37} = \frac{6 \times 37}{1 \times 37} = \frac{6}{1} \times \frac{37}{37} = 6 \times 1 = 6$$

2.0 FRACTIONS (continued)

Exercise 2.1

1. Express the fraction represented by the shaded part in the figure below.

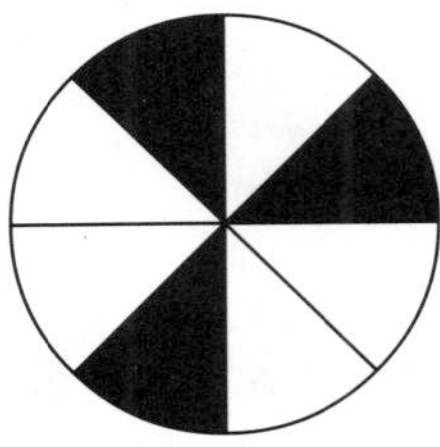

2. Illustrate $\frac{7}{10}$ using a rectangle representing the whole similar to the previous exercise.

3. Write a fraction to represent the shaded area.

Reduce the following fractions to the lowest terms if possible.

4. $\frac{10}{12} = ?$

5. $\frac{21}{12} = ?$

6. $\frac{15}{26} = ?$

7. $\frac{33}{121} = ?$

8. $\frac{308}{187} = ?$

9. $\frac{3{,}150}{4{,}158} = ?$

10. $\frac{286}{858} = ?$

11. $\frac{25}{80} = ?$

Use unity fractions to convert the following units of measure.

12. 12 ft. = ? yd. (1 yd. = 3 ft.)

13. 2 gal. = ? qt. (4 qt. = 1 gal.)

14. 2 gal. = ? oz. (1 qt . = 32 oz.)

15. 18,000 sec. = ? hr. (1 hr. = 60 min., & 1 min. = 60 sec.)

16. 15,840 ft. = ? mi. (1 mi. = 5,280 ft.)

Convert the following mixed numbers to improper fractions.

17. $7\frac{1}{4} = ?$

18. $6\frac{1}{7} = ?$

19. $4\frac{8}{9} = ?$

20. $4\frac{3}{11} = ?$

21. $7\frac{1}{8} = ?$

22. $9\frac{2}{7} = ?$

23. $2\frac{7}{8} = ?$

24. $5\frac{1}{13} = ?$

Convert the following improper fractions to mixed numbers.

25. $\frac{49}{5} = ?$

26. $\frac{100}{3} = ?$

27. $\frac{31}{4} = ?$

28. $\frac{8}{3} = ?$

29. $\frac{53}{7} = ?$

30. $\frac{55}{6} = ?$

31. $\frac{267}{11} = ?$

32. $\frac{436}{11} = ?$

2.0 FRACTIONS (continued)

2.2 Addition of Like Fractions

When adding two or more like fractions, we simply add their numerators and write the sum over the common denominator.

Example 1.

Add $\frac{2}{11}$ and $\frac{5}{11}$. $\quad \frac{2}{11} + \frac{5}{11} = \frac{7}{11}$

EXERCISE 2.2

Add each set of like fractions below and simplify your sum if possible. Express any improper fractions as mixed numbers:

1. $\frac{1}{5} + \frac{2}{5} = ?$

2. $\frac{3}{22} + \frac{5}{22} = ?$

3. $\frac{3}{17} + \frac{4}{17} + \frac{5}{17} = ?$

4. $\frac{10}{19} + \frac{2}{19} + \frac{15}{19} = ?$

5. $\frac{7}{8} + \frac{2}{8} + \frac{5}{8} = ?$

6. $\frac{1}{7} + \frac{3}{7} + \frac{5}{7} + \frac{6}{7} = ?$

7. $\frac{2}{5} + 1\frac{3}{5} = ?$ *HINT:* First change the mixed mumber to an improper fraction.

$$1\frac{3}{5} = \frac{5}{8}$$

2.3 Lowest Common Denominator

When adding two or more unlike fractions, we must first find a *lowest common denominator* (LCD). The LCD is the smallest whole number that is exactly divisible by all of the denominators.

Example 1. Find the LCD of the fractions $\frac{1}{15}, \frac{1}{5}$, and $\frac{1}{8}$.

The LCD is 120, because 120 is the smallest whole number divisible by 5, 8, and 15.

We cannot always determine the LCD by inspection. Before we look at the procedure it is important to understand what is meant by a *prime number.* A prime number is a whole number whose only factors are 1 and itself. For example, 2, 3, 5, 7, and 11 are prime numbers. Two or more numbers being multiplied are called *factors.* Note that 6 is not a prime number because it has factors other than 1 and 6, namely 2 and 3. Whole numbers that are not prime are called *composite.*

The procedure for finding an LCD is as follows:

1. Factor each denominator into its prime factors; that is, factor each number completely.

2. For each prime factor, look for the denominator in which it appears the most times. Write each factor the number of times it appears most in any one denominator in step 1.

3. Multiply together the prime factors listed in step 2. The product is the LCD.

2.0 FRACTIONS (continued)

Example 2. Find the LCD of $\frac{4}{27}$ and $\frac{5}{18}$.

STEP 1 $27 = 3 \times 9$
$= 3 \times 3 \times 3$
$18 = 2 \times 9$
$= 2 \times 3 \times 3$

STEP 2 $(3 \times 3 \times 3) \times (2)$

STEP 3 $3 \times 3 \times 3 \times 2 = 54$

The LCD is 54.

EXERCISE 2.3

Find the LCD for each of the sets of fractions.

1. $\frac{3}{8}, \frac{2}{5}$

2. $\frac{4}{7}, \frac{1}{3}, \frac{17}{49}$

3. $\frac{5}{27}, \frac{2}{3}, \frac{11}{12}$

2.4 Addition of Unlike Fractions

Suppose we want to add $\frac{4}{5}$ and $\frac{2}{3}$. Since these fractions are unlike, we must first change them to equivalent fractions that have a common denominator. This means that we need to find the LCD of 5 and 3. The LCD is 15. We then convert $\frac{4}{5}$ into an equivalent fraction having a denominator of 15. We do the same with $\frac{2}{3}$.

$\frac{4}{5} = \frac{12}{15}$ and $\frac{2}{3} = \frac{10}{12}$

We then add the equivalent fractions.

$$\frac{4}{5} + \frac{2}{3} = \frac{12}{15} + \frac{10}{12}$$

$$= \frac{12 + 15}{15}$$

$$= \frac{22}{15}, \text{ or } 1\frac{7}{15}$$

Note that when we convert $\frac{4}{5}$ to $\frac{12}{15}$ we are simply multiplying $\frac{4}{5}$ by 1, but 1 is written as $\frac{3}{3}$. Multiplying any number by 1 doesn't change its value, but it may change its appearance.

$$\frac{4}{5} = \frac{4}{5} \times 1$$

$$= \frac{4}{5} \times \frac{3}{3}$$

$$= \frac{4 \times 3}{5 \times 3}$$

$$= \frac{12}{15}$$

Example 1. Add $\frac{1}{8}$ and $\frac{5}{32}$.

Find the LCD: 32

$$\frac{1}{8} + \frac{5}{32} = \frac{4}{32} + \frac{5}{32}$$

$$= \frac{9}{32}$$

Example 2. Add $\frac{5}{18}$ and $\frac{11}{12}$.

Find the LCD.

$$18 = 2 \times 3 \times 3$$

$$12 = 2 \times 2 \times 3$$

$$\text{LCD} = 2 \times 2 \times 3 \times 3$$

$$= 36$$

$$\frac{5}{18} + \frac{11}{12} = \frac{10}{36} + \frac{33}{36}$$

$$= \frac{43}{36}, \text{ or } 1\frac{7}{36}$$

2.0 FRACTIONS (continued)

EXERCISE 2.4

Add each of the following unlike fractions and express your answer in simplest form.

1. $\frac{2}{9} + \frac{5}{18} = ?$

2. $\frac{2}{5} + \frac{5}{6} + \frac{1}{2} = ?$

3. $\frac{2}{15} + \frac{3}{4} + \frac{1}{16} = ?$

4. $\frac{2}{3} + \frac{3}{5} + \frac{5}{7} + \frac{7}{9} = ?$

5. If a share of stock gained $\frac{5}{8}$ of a point during one day of trading and $\frac{3}{7}$ of a point on the next day of trading, how many points did the stock gain during those two days?

6. Two adjacent house lots are $\frac{3}{5}$ and $\frac{3}{4}$ acres in size. What is the total amount of acreage?

7. $\frac{15}{17} + \frac{3}{17} = ?$

8. $\frac{2}{3} + \frac{1}{2} + \frac{5}{6} = ?$

9. $\frac{5}{18} + \frac{11}{12} = ?$

10. $\frac{3}{7} + \frac{5}{7} + \frac{7}{9} + \frac{2}{3} = ?$

11. $3\frac{1}{2} + 2\frac{1}{3} = ?$

12. $6\frac{2}{3} + 8\frac{2}{3} = ?$

13. $11\frac{1}{9} + 3 = ?$

14. $4\frac{3}{5} + \frac{1}{2} = ?$

15. $9\frac{2}{7} + 4\frac{3}{4} = ?$

16. $3\frac{1}{4} + 2\frac{1}{3} + 4\frac{3}{5} = ?$

17. Newspaper ads are sold by the column inch (c.i.). How many total number of column inches are there in the following ads of $6\frac{1}{2}$, $5\frac{3}{4}$, and 3 column inches?

2.5 Subtraction of Fractions

The process of subtracting fractions is similar to the addition of fractions. To subtract like fractions, simply subtract the smaller numerator from the larger numerator, place the difference over the common denominator and simplify if possible.

Example 1. Subtract $\frac{17}{32}$ from $\frac{5}{32}$.

$$\frac{17}{32} - \frac{5}{32} = \frac{17-5}{32} = \frac{12}{32}, \text{ or } \frac{3}{8}$$

Example 2. Subtract $\frac{7}{13}$ from $\frac{12}{13}$.

$$\frac{12}{13} - \frac{7}{13} = \frac{12-7}{13} = \frac{5}{13}$$

If we are subtracting unlike fractions, we must first find the LCD, just as we did when adding unlike fractions.

Example 3. Subtract $\frac{4}{11}$ from $\frac{3}{9}$.

The LCD is 99.

$$\frac{4}{11} - \frac{3}{9} = \frac{36}{99} - \frac{33}{99} = \frac{36-33}{99}$$

$$= \frac{3}{99} = \frac{1}{33}$$

Example 4. Subtract $\frac{7}{5}$ from $\frac{21}{13}$.

The LCD is 65.

$$\frac{21}{13} - \frac{7}{5} = \frac{105}{65} - \frac{91}{65} = \frac{105-91}{65}$$

$$= \frac{14}{65}$$

EXERCISE 2.5

Subtract the following fractions:

1. $\frac{11}{17} - \frac{5}{17} = ?$
2. $\frac{21}{13} - \frac{7}{5} = ?$
3. $\frac{10}{17} - \frac{5}{11} = ?$
4. In a new business condominium, $\frac{2}{3}$ of the building is occupied by the Ajax Hardware Co., and $\frac{1}{5}$ of the building is occupied by Belair Realty. How much of the building is *not* occupied?

2.0 FRACTIONS (continued)

5. $\frac{9}{16} - \frac{4}{16} = ?$

6. $\frac{5}{12} - \frac{1}{3} = ?$

7. $\frac{1}{2} - \frac{3}{6} = ?$

8. $5\frac{1}{3} - 2\frac{7}{8} = ?$

9. $39\frac{1}{6} - \frac{5}{7} = ?$

10. $17\frac{11}{13} - 9 = ?$

11. $\left(5\frac{1}{3} - 3\frac{1}{4}\right) + 4\frac{1}{5} = ?$

12. $7\frac{2}{9} - \left(1\frac{7}{8} + 3\frac{1}{4}\right) = ?$

(*HINT:* Perform operations within parentheses first.)

2.6 Multiplication of Fractions

There is no need to find an LCD when we multiply fractions. To find the product of two fractions, first multiply their numerators. This product will be the numerator of the new fraction. Then multiply their denominators. This product will be the denominator of the new fraction. If it is possible to reduce your answer to lower terms, do so.

In general:

$$\frac{a}{b} \times \frac{c}{d} = \frac{a \times c}{b \times d}$$

where b and d do not equal zero.

Example 1. Graphically we can show the multiplication of a fraction by a fraction such as $\frac{2}{3} \times \frac{3}{7} = \frac{2}{7}$.

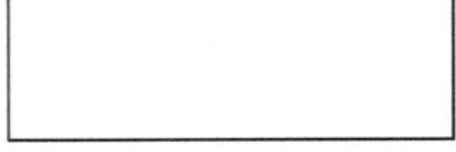

1 whole

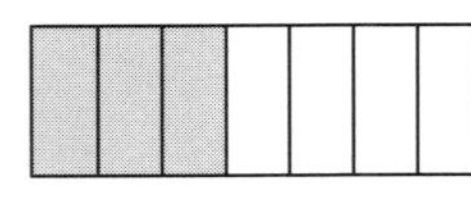

$\frac{3}{7}$ of 1 whole

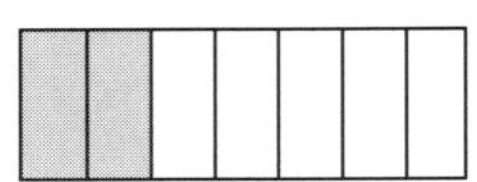

$\frac{2}{3}$ of $\frac{3}{7}$ of 1 whole

$$\frac{2}{3} \times \frac{3}{7} = \frac{2}{7}$$

Example 2. $\frac{1}{2} \times \frac{1}{3} = \frac{1}{6}$

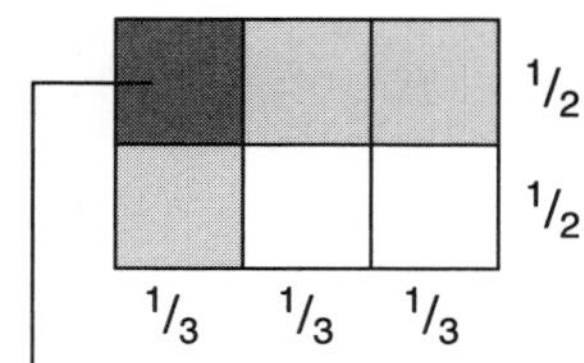

Example 3. Multiply $\frac{2}{9}$ by $\frac{5}{14}$.

$$\frac{2}{9} \times \frac{5}{14} = \frac{2 \times 5}{9 \times 14} = \frac{10}{126} = \frac{5}{63}$$ reduced to lowest terms

Example 4. Multiply $\frac{4}{5}$ by $3\frac{3}{8}$. ***HINT:*** First convert the mixed number to an improper fraction.

$$3\frac{3}{8} = \frac{27}{8}$$

$$\frac{4}{5} \times \frac{27}{8} = \frac{4 \times 27}{5 \times 8} = \frac{27}{10}$$

EXERCISE 2.6

Multiply each of the following fractions and express your answer in simplest form. ***HINT:*** Perform operation in parentheses first:

1. $\frac{1}{5} \times \frac{2}{7} = ?$

2. $\frac{5}{13} \times \frac{4}{9} = ?$

3. $\frac{6}{7} \times \left(\frac{2}{9} + \frac{3}{4}\right) = ?$

4. $\frac{3}{8} \times \frac{2}{5} = ?$

5. $\frac{1}{2} \times \frac{5}{6} = ?$

6. $\frac{5}{6} \times \frac{2}{15} = ?$

2.0 FRACTIONS (continued)

7. $\frac{5}{12} \times \frac{42}{65} = ?$

8. $\frac{8}{3} \times \frac{21}{32} = ?$

9. $9 \times 3\frac{1}{3} = ?$

10. $5\frac{2}{3} \times 12 = ?$

11. $2\frac{1}{5} \times \frac{5}{22} = ?$

12. $3\frac{1}{7} \times 2\frac{1}{8} = ?$

13. $4\frac{7}{8} \times 0 = ?$

14. $5\frac{3}{8} \times 6\frac{2}{5} = ?$

15. $\frac{16}{85} \times \frac{125}{84} = ?$

16. $\frac{3}{7} \times \left(\frac{4}{5} + \frac{3}{4}\right) = ?$

17. $\left(\frac{2}{9} - \frac{1}{7}\right) \times \left(\frac{1}{3} + \frac{2}{5}\right) = ?$

18. $\frac{5}{7} \times \frac{14}{25} \times \frac{21}{28} = ?$

A recipe will provide not only the ingredients, but also the number of servings it yields. We can use the multiplication of fractions to change the number of servings. If a recipe has a yield of six servings and we are serving eight we simply multiply each ingredient by the fraction $\frac{8}{6}$ or $\frac{4}{3}$.

19. Find the amounts of ingredients needed to make light corn custard for nine servings when the ingredients below will serve four.

2 cups corn kernels	1 tsp. salt
4 eggs	$\frac{1}{4}$ tsp. ground white pepper
1 cup cream	Dash nutmeg
1 Tb sugar	2 Tb melted butter

2.7 Division of Fractions

When we divide by a fraction, we first invert the fraction. We then multiply by the inverted fraction. In general,

$$\frac{a}{b} \div \frac{c}{d} = \frac{a}{b} \times \frac{d}{c}$$

if b, c, and d are not equal to zero.

Example 1. Divide $\frac{2}{3}$ by $\frac{3}{5}$.

$$\frac{2}{3} \div \frac{3}{5} = \frac{2}{3} \times \frac{5}{3} = \frac{10}{9}, \text{ or } 1\frac{1}{9}$$

Let's consider the above example in more detail. We can write $\frac{2}{3} \div \frac{3}{5}$ as $(\frac{2}{3} \div \frac{3}{5}) \times 1$.

Remember that 1 multiplied times any number is that number. And since 1 is any nonzero number divided by itself, we can replace the 1 with $(\frac{5}{3} \div \frac{5}{3})$

Therefore,

$$\frac{2}{3} \div \frac{3}{5} = \left(\frac{2}{3} \div \frac{3}{5}\right) \times \left(\frac{5}{3} \div \frac{5}{3}\right) = \frac{\frac{2}{3}}{\frac{3}{5}} \times \frac{\frac{5}{3}}{\frac{5}{3}}$$

But $\frac{3}{5} \times \frac{5}{3} = \frac{15}{15} = 1$. Therefore,

$$\frac{2}{3} \div \frac{3}{5} = \frac{\frac{2}{3} \times \frac{3}{5}}{1} = \frac{2}{3} \times \frac{3}{5}$$

Example 2. How many $\frac{1}{2}$s are there in 3?

$3 \div \frac{1}{2} = ?,\quad 3 \times \frac{2}{1} = 6$ There are six $\frac{1}{2}$s in 3.

Graphically the above can be shown as:

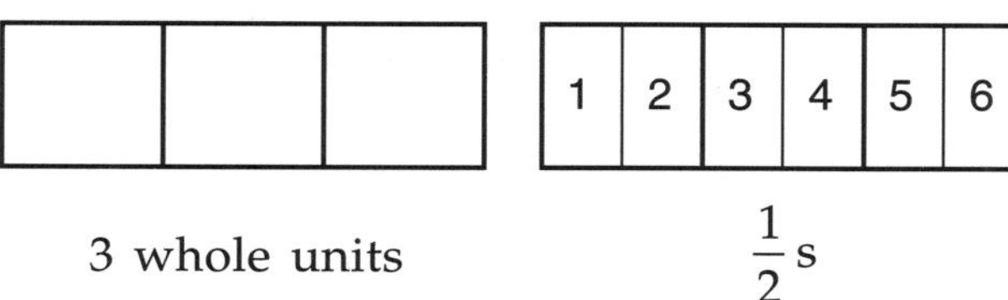

3 whole units $\frac{1}{2}$s

2.0 FRACTIONS (continued)

Example 3. Divide $\frac{3}{7}$ by $\frac{1}{4}$.

$$\frac{3}{7} \div \frac{1}{4} = \frac{3}{7} \times \frac{4}{1} = \frac{12}{7}, \text{ or } 1\frac{5}{7}$$

Example 4. Divide $\frac{21}{25}$ by $\frac{3}{5}$.

$$\frac{21}{25} \div \frac{3}{5} = \frac{21}{25} \times \frac{5}{3} = \frac{105}{75} = \frac{7}{5}, \text{ or } 1\frac{2}{5}$$

It would be useful to simplify our numbers before we multiplied:

$$\frac{21}{25} \div \frac{3}{5} = \frac{21}{25} \times \frac{5}{3} = \frac{7}{5} \times \frac{1}{1} = \frac{7}{5}$$

Example 5. Divide $\frac{7}{3}$ by $3\frac{1}{3}$.

$$\frac{7}{3} \div 3\frac{1}{3} = \frac{7}{3} \div \frac{10}{3} = \frac{7}{3} \times \frac{3}{10} = \frac{21}{30} = \frac{7}{10}$$

EXERCISE 2.7

Divide each of the following fractions and express your answer in simplest form:

1. $\frac{2}{3} \div \frac{1}{2}$

2. $\frac{18}{25} \div 4 \left(\text{recall that } 4 = \frac{4}{1}\right)$

3. $\frac{0}{7} \div \frac{5}{17}$

4. $\frac{3}{4} \div \frac{0}{2}$

5. $\frac{3}{7} \div \frac{2}{3}$

6. $\frac{3}{5} \div \frac{12}{25}$

7. $8 \div \frac{3}{4}$

8. $\frac{3}{4} \div 8$

9. $\frac{3}{8} \div 2\frac{3}{4}$

10. $\left(3\frac{2}{7} \div 4\frac{1}{9}\right) \div 2\frac{5}{7}$

11. $7\frac{1}{9} \div \left(\frac{6}{7} \div 7\frac{1}{6}\right)$

3.0 DECIMALS

We encounter decimals each time we make a purchase or receive a paycheck. Companies conducting business with foreign countries need to have a knowledge of decimals when converting to metric measures or when using foreign currency. The operations of addition, subtraction, multiplication, and division are all applicable to decimal numbers.

If a decimal number is greater than one, say 23.45, we read the digits to the left of the decimal point as whole numbers. The decimal point is read as "and," and the place value of the extreme right digit is the denominator. Thus, 23.45 is read as "23 and 45 hundredths." Alternatively, we can read it as "twenty-three point four five."

Example 1. Write these decimals in words: (a) 12.3; (b) 1.23; (c) 0.123; (d) $14.35

(a) 12.3 is twelve and three-tenths.

(b) 1.23 is one and twenty-three hundreths.

(c) 0.123 is one hundred twenty-three thousandths.

(d) $14.35 is fourteen dollars, thirty-five cents.

Example 2. 0.94 liter equals 1 quart.

Example 3. 2.54 centimeters equals 1 inch.

Example 4. 1 German mark = 0.6767 of 1 U.S. dollar.

3.0 DECIMALS (continued)

3.1 Converting Fractions to Decimals

Any fraction can be expressed as a decimal by simply dividing the denominator into the numerator.

Example 1. Use a calculator to convert these fractions to decimals: (a) $\frac{3}{5}$, (b) $\frac{11}{17}$, and (c) $\frac{1}{3}$.

(a) [3] [÷] [5] [=] *0.6*

(b) [11] [÷] [17] [=] *0.6470588*

(c) [1] [÷] [3] [=] *0.3333333*

The latter is called a repeating decimal.

EXERCISE 3.1

Convert each of the following fractions to an equivalent decimal number. Express answers correct to the nearest hundredth:

1. $\frac{4}{5}$

2. $8\frac{3}{4}$

3. $\frac{7}{500}$

4. $\frac{87}{100}$

5. $72\frac{11}{25}$

6. $\frac{5}{9}$

7. $\frac{1}{3}$

8. $\frac{1}{4}$

9. $\frac{9}{10}$

10. $\frac{25}{32}$

11. $\frac{27}{135}$

12. $\frac{7}{9}$

3.2 Converting Decimals to Fractions

If any common fraction can be changed to an equivalent decimal number, isn't it reasonable to assume that any decimal number could be changed to a common fraction? If $\frac{3}{5} = 0.6$, then $0.6 = \frac{3}{5}$. Since 0.6 is six-tenths,

$$0.6 = \frac{6}{10} = \frac{3}{5}$$

We can change any decimal fraction to its equivalent common fraction by first determining the place value of the digit on the extreme right, and using that value as the denominator of our common fraction. For example, in

0.24

4's place value is hundredths. Thus, the denominator of our fraction is 100. The digits in the decimal fraction, in this case 24, is the numerator of your fraction. Hence,

$$0.24 = \frac{24}{100}, \text{ which can be reduced to } \frac{6}{25}$$

Similarly,

$$0.625 = \frac{625}{1,000}, \quad \text{or} \quad \frac{5}{8} \qquad \text{and} \qquad 5.13 = \frac{513}{100}$$

EXERCISE 3.2

Convert each of the following decimal fractions to an equivalent common fraction in simplest form:

1. 0.002

2. 1.65 (***Hint:*** $1\frac{65}{100}$)

3. 0.09

4. 0.17

5. 0.123

6. 2.3

7. 17.06

8. 0.0037

9. 260.26

10. 0.871

11. 3.75

12. 2.006

3.0 DECIMALS (continued)

3.3 Adding Decimal Numbers

Adding decimal numbers is not much different from adding whole numbers. We need to arrange the decimal numbers under each other, keeping the decimal points aligned in a vertical column, if we are not using a calculator. Once this is done, add as if they were whole numbers.

For example, add the following: 2.134 + 51.02 + 0.0394

$$\begin{array}{r} 2.134 \\ 51.02 \\ +\ \ 0.0394 \\ \hline 53.1934 \end{array}$$

EXERCISE 3.3

Add the following decimal numbers. Check your answers using your calculator:

1. 1.234 + 12.34 + 123.4 + 123

2. Tom needs to pay the following monthly bills: rent, $289; car payment, $137.49; groceries, $201.35; E-Z credit card payment, $72.12. What is Tom's total monthly payment?

3. The following deposits were made in a local environmental organization's bank account: $463.62, $74.89, $111.10, and $59.89. If the account had a previous balance of $1,593.43, what is the new balance?

4. 0.286 + 8.76 + 59.6 = ?

5. $$\begin{array}{r} 8.37 \\ 34.103 \\ +\ 9.2376 \\ \hline \end{array}$$

6. At the beginning of the fall semester at the Tech College, Dick spent $850.60 for tuition, $287.39 for books, $630.50 for meals, and $785.90 for a room. Find the total cost of Dick's fall semester.

7. Lorraine's checking account balance was $1,650.37 at the beginning of the month. She made the following deposits: $117.10, $23.07, $331.14, and $202.49. What is Lorraine's new balance?

8. A salesman records his daily mileage to be included in his expense report at the end of the week. The following mileages were recorded; 79.3 miles, 114.8 miles, 88.3 miles, 157.8 miles, and 91.6 miles. How many miles did he drive altogether?

9. Juan is training for a swimming meet. How many kilometers did he swim if during the past three days he swam 4.2 (km) kilometers, 520 (m) meters and 2.8 (km) kilometers? ***NOTE:*** 1 km = 1,000 m.

3.4 Subtracting Decimal Numbers

Just as in the addition of decimal numbers, we must align the decimal points when we subtract decimal numbers.

Example 1. Subtract: 123.45 from 15.7.

$$\begin{array}{r} 123.45 \\ -\ 15.7 \\ \hline 107.75 \end{array}$$

Example 2. Subtract 0.69 – 0.3111.

First arrange vertically, with the decimal points aligned. Then subtract.

$$\begin{array}{l} 0.69 \\ -\ 0.3111 \\ \hline 0.3789 \end{array}$$

3.0 DECIMALS (continued)

EXERCISE 3.4

Subtract the following decimal numbers. Check your answers using your calculator:

1. 12.34 – 8.09 = ?

2. 37 – 1.503 = ?

3. 529.13 – 89.709 = ?

4. John's temperature reading is 102.7° Fahrenheit. Normal body temperature is 98.6° Fahrenheit. How much above normal is John's temperature?

5. What is the current value of a stock in Company A if it was originally purchased at $16.23 per share and the price dropped in value by $.57 per share?

6. $\begin{array}{r} 67.93502 \\ -\ 53.07035 \\ \hline \end{array}$

7. How much change would you receive from a $50 bill if you made a purchase of $31.33?

8. If a microwave oven that regularly sells for $429.95 is marked down $72.50, what is the sale price?

9. Phil put 30¢ in a parking meter at 12:23 p.m. By what time must he return if 10¢ allows him to park for $\frac{1}{2}$ hour?

3.5 Rounding Off Decimal Numbers

The rule for rounding off decimal numbers is similar to the rule for rounding off whole numbers.

Example 1. Round 0.32 to the nearest tenth.

STEP 1 Underline the tenths digit: $0.\underline{3}21$

STEP 2 Look at the digit immediately to the right (the hundredths digit). This digit is 2, which is less than 5, so the underlined digit is not changed.

STEP 3 Discard the digits to the right of the underlined digit: $0.\underline{3}$.

Note that step 3 is different when rounding off decimal numbers. We discard the digits to the right of the underlined digit, instead of replacing them with zeros. If we expressed our rounded-off number as 0.300, it would be rounded to thousandths, not tenths.

Example 2. Round 5.0632 to the nearest hundredth.

$5.0632 \approx 5.06$ The symbol $\approx$ is read as "approximately equal to"

Example 3. Round 17.6666, to the nearest thousandth.

$17.6666 \approx 17.667$

Example 4. Fluctuations in the world's economy create changes in the value of the U.S. dollar. If the value of a Canadian dollar is 0.7613 that of a U.S. dollar, then \$45 U.S. equals how many Canadian dollars? (***HINT:*** We use unity fractions to solve this problem.)

\$45 U.S. = ? Canadian dollars

$$\$45\,\frac{(0.7613\text{ C})}{\$1\text{ U.S.}} = \$34.26\text{ Canadian}$$

3.0 DECIMALS (continued)

One note of caution! In many real-life situations the rule for rounding off decimals will not apply. If you plan to mail a letter that weighs 1.3 ounces, the post office will charge you for 2 ounces, not for 1 ounce. If the price of three cans of soup is $1.00 and you buy only one can, you will pay 34 cents, not 33 cents.

EXERCISE 3.5

1. Round 3.456 to the nearest tenth.
2. Round 0.00999 to the nearest thousandth.
3. Round 14.5679873 to the nearest millionth.
4. Round 5.00873 to the nearest hundredth.
5. Round 2.00500 to the nearest hundredth.
6. Round 1.849 to the nearest hundredth.
7. Round 14.049 to the nearest tenth.
8. Round 0.24687 to the nearest ten-thousandth.

3.6 Multiplying Decimal Numbers

It isn't necessary to align decimal points when multiplying decimal numbers. Multiplying decimal numbers is done in the same way as for whole numbers. The number of decimal places in the product is equal to the sum of the decimal places in each factor.

Example 1. Multiply 34.75 by 0.123.

$$\begin{array}{rl} 34.75 & \text{2 decimal places} \\ \times\ \ 0.123 & \text{3 decimal places} \\ \hline 4.27425 & 2 + 3 = 5 \text{ decimal places} \end{array}$$

Example 2. Use a calculator to multiply 34.75 by 0.123.

[34.75] [×] [0.123] [=] *4.27425*

EXERCISE 3.6

Multiply the following decimal numbers:

1. 23.17 × 100 = ?

2. 89.794 × 3.72 = ?

3. At the local service station the selling price of regular unleaded gasoline is $1.049 per gallon. If you buy 13.3 gallons of gasoline, how much do you pay?

4. The state income tax on your business is $504 plus 0.06 times your profit. If your profit last year was $13,689, what amount of income tax did you owe?

5. 0.0123 × 1.08 = ?

6. If your mortgage payments are $723.50 per month, what is the total amount of the payments for 25 years?

7. How many miles would you drive in one five-day work week if the distance from your home to your work is 19.7 miles? (Consider the distance to and from work.)

8. If three apples sell for .79 cents, how much will $1\frac{1}{2}$ dozen apples cost?

9. If the annual interest rate for borrowing money was 0.094 times the sum of money borrowed, find the interest on a loan of $4,400 over three years.

10. Phillip is paid $8.50 an hour for a 40-hour work week and 1.5 times the regular rate for overtime. How much gross pay would be received for a week in which he worked 45 hours?

11. If a new car loses 0.31 of its value during the first year, how much would an $11,370 car be worth at the end of one year?

3.0 DECIMALS (continued)

12. A nurse will most frequently use liter (L) and milliliter (mL) as units of measure. The prefix milli means 0.001 of a unit. Thus, 0.001L = 1 mL and 1L = 100 mL.

a. 1.75L = ? mL

b. 0.33L = ? mL

c. 23.694L = ? mL

13. Find the freight charge for shipping 225 television sets if each television set weighs 68.5 kg and the charge is $9 per 100 kg. Round the quotient up to the nearest whole number.

3.7 Dividing Decimal Numbers

Dividing decimal numbers is almost the same as dividing whole numbers, except that we must first make the divisor a whole number. To do this, we move the decimal point until it is to the right of the last digit in the divisor. Then we must move the decimal point in the dividend the same number of places to the right as we did in the divisor. The decimal point in the quotient is placed directly over the decimal point in the dividend.

Example 1. Divide 1.5328 by 0.13.

STEP 1 Make the divisor a whole number.

0.13 → 13

We moved the decimal point two places to the right.

STEP 2 Adjust the dividend accordingly.

1.5328 → 153.28

STEP 3 Divide, adding zeros to the dividend as necessary. The decimal point in the quotient is directly over the decimal point in the dividend.

$13\overline{)153.280000}$ = 11.790769, or 11.791 rounded to the nearest thousandth

EXERCISE 3.7

Divide the following decimal numbers. Round off your answers to the nearest hundredth.

1. 15.7 ÷ 2.5 = ?

2. 0.76543 ÷ 100 = ?

3. 1360.997 ÷ 1.1112 = ?

4. James received an inheritance of $45,350 from his uncle's estate. If James' inheritance represents 0.7 of his uncle's total estate, what was the total value of the estate?

5. 0.23401 ÷ 6.9 = ?

6. 0.2307 ÷ 26.7= ?

7. When converting from milliliters to liters, divide the number of milliliters by 1,000. Convert the following to liters:

   a. 1,5000 mL = ? L

   b. 1.35 mL = ? L

   c. 860 mL = ? L

8. If 1 Mexican peso equals 0.15369 in U.S. dollars, what is the equivalent of 5,000 Mexican pesos in U.S. dollars?

9. Federal guidelines now established enable us to determine a standard way of describing obesity using a *body mass index* (BMI).

   A BMI measurement of less than 25 suggests that you are not overweight. BMI is equal to body weight in kilograms divided by height in meters squared.

3.0 DECIMALS (continued)

Procedure for determining your BMI:

STEP 1 Multiply your weight in pounds by 0.45 to get kilograms.

STEP 2 Take your height in inches and multiply this number by 0.0254 to get meters.

STEP 3 Multiply the number in step 2 by itself.

STEP 4 Divide the number in step 3 into your weight in kilograms.

Example: A man who is 5′9″ tall and weighs 160 pounds has a BMI = 23.4.

$$\text{BMI} = \frac{160(0.45)}{[69(0.0254)]^2} = \frac{72}{3.07\ldots}, \text{ or } 23.4$$

a. Find the BMI of a woman 5′ 4″ tall who weighs 145 pounds.

b. Find the BMI of a man 5′ 2″ tall who weighs 230 pounds.

10. A retail management trainee earns $21,560.30 for a year's work. How much does she earn in one month?

11. Gasoline tax is $0.16 per gallon. How many gallons of gasoline were used if $21.34 was paid in taxes?

12. A shopping mall rented 48,862.5 square feet of space for $114,826,875. How much was received for each square foot?

13. Heating oil sells for $1.69 per gallon. Charles received a bill from the oil company for $401.21. How many gallons of oil were delivered?

14. Which is a better buy: a $\frac{1}{2}$-inch, 40-foot hose costing $7.20 or a $\frac{1}{2}$-inch, 60-foot hose costing $10.49?

4.0 PERCENT

A *percentage* is a fraction whose denominator is 100. Twenty-five percent, or 25%, means 25 parts out of 100. Percentages are frequently expressed as decimals. For example, 25 percent can be written as 0.25.

To convert a decimal to a percentage, move the decimal point two places to the right and add the percent sign.

Example 1. Convert (a) 0.35, (b) 0.05, and (c) 12.73 to percentages.

a. 0.35 = 35%

b. 0.05 = 5%

c. 12.73 = 1.273%

To convert a percentage to a decimal, drop the percent sign and move the decimal point two places to the left.

Example 2. Convert (a) 35%, (b) 15.5%, and (c) 125% to decimals.

a. 35% = 0.35

b. 15.5% = 0.155

c. 125% = 1.25

To convert a fraction to a percentage, first change the fraction to a decimal, then move the decimal point two places to the right and add the percent sign.

Example 3. Convert (a) $\frac{1}{5}$, (b) $\frac{3}{8}$, and (c) $2\frac{3}{5}$ to percentages.

a. $\frac{1}{5} = 0.20 = 20\%$

b. $\frac{3}{8} = 0.375 = 37.5\%$

c. $2\frac{3}{5} = \frac{13}{5} = 2.60 = 260\%$

Note that in (c) we first changed the mixed number to an improper fraction.

To convert a percentage to a fraction, drop the percent sign, place the number over 100, and simplify if possible.

4.0 PERCENT (continued)

Example 4. Convert (a) 50%, (b) 130%, and (c) $16\frac{2}{3}\%$ to fractions and reduce to lowest terms.

a. $50\% = \frac{50}{100} = \frac{1}{2}$

b. $130\% = \frac{130}{100} = \frac{13}{10}$

c. $16\frac{2}{3}\% = \frac{16\frac{2}{3}}{100} = \frac{50/3}{100} = \frac{50}{3} \times \frac{1}{100} = \frac{50}{300} = \frac{1}{6}$

Note that in (c) we had a numerator that was a mixed number. If the numerator of a fraction is a fraction, decimal, or mixed number, we have a *complex fraction*. These complex fractions need to be simplified so that ultimately both the numerator and denominator are whole numbers.

Example 5. A first-place team in baseball has the highest won–lost percentage.

$$\text{Won–lost percentage} = \frac{\text{Number of wins}}{\text{Games played}}$$

If Oakland won 30 games and lost 56 games, its won–lost percentage is approximately 34.9%.

$$\text{Won–lost percentage} = \frac{30}{30 + 56} = 0.3488, \text{ or } 34.9\%$$

EXERCISE 4.0

Convert the following decimals to percents:

1. 111.05

2. 0.0045

3. 0.03

4. 0.31

5. 0.0554

6. 125

7. 93.2

8. 45.67

9. 0.02

10. 0.99

11. To change pounds to kilograms (kg) (1,000 grams), divide the number of pounds by 2.2. Thus, 220 lbs. = $\frac{220}{2.2}$, or 100 kg.

    How many kilograms are in the number of pounds below?

    a. 44 lbs. = ? kg

    b. 198 lbs. = ? kg

12. 

    Express the shaded part of the square as a percentage.

13. Determine what percentage the shaded part is of the whole.

Convert the following percentages to decimals:

14. 93%

15. 0.0025%

16. 83%

17. 150%

18. 16.4%

19. 0.45%

20. 101%

Convert the following fractions to percentages:

21. $\frac{9}{5}$

22. $\frac{537}{1,000}$

Convert the following percentages to fractions and simplify:

23. 81.65%

24. 400.1%

25. $16\frac{2}{3}\%$

26. $11\frac{1}{9}\%$

27. $8\frac{2}{3}\%$

28. $\frac{1}{8}\%$

29. 205%

P A R T

II

Basic Applications

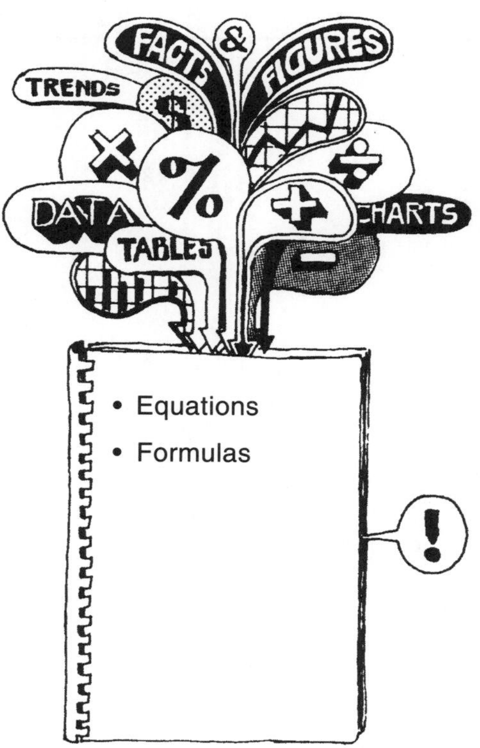

HINT:

Your calculator may have the following fraction key, [$a\frac{b}{c}$].

This key enables you to perform operations with fractions. For example, to enter $\frac{5}{6}$ into your calculator press the following keys:

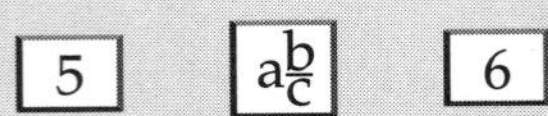

Your display will show 5⌐— 6 or 5 —┘6 depending on the manufacturer of your calculator. NOTE that the fraction has not been converted to its equivalent decimal notation.

5.0 EQUATIONS

An *equation* is a statement that two mathematical expressions are equal. For example, $3 + 5 = 8$ and $x + 7 = 11$ are equations. In the second example, x is called a *variable,* or an unknown, and 7 and 11 are called *constants.* You do not need to know much mathematics to guess that x has to have a value such that adding x to 7 will give 11. That is, $x = 4$.

Example 1. Solve $3x + 1 = 13$.
If $x = 2$, then $(3 \times 2) + 1 =$

$$6 + 1 = 7$$
$$7 \neq 13 \quad \text{(That is, 7 does not equal 13.)}$$

Therefore $x \neq 2$.

If $x = 4$, then $(3 \times 4) + 1 =$

$$12 + 1 = 13$$
$$13 = 13$$

But guessing is not an efficient way to solve equations. We need a set of rules to solve equations without guessing. To *solve* an equation means to find the value of the variable that will make the equation a true statement.*

We have solved the equation. The solution to the equation is that $x = 4$.

There are five basic rules we need to know in order to solve an equation. These rules specify changes we can make to both sides of an equation so that they remain equal; these changes help us solve the equation by isolating the variable.

Sometimes several of the rules may have to be used to solve an equation. When we solve an equation we wish to *isolate* the variable. That is, we want to get the unknown alone on one side of the equation.

RULE 1 The same number may be added to both sides of an equation.

a. $3 + 8 = 11$ $\quad 3 + 8 + 2 = 11 + 2 \quad 13 = 13$

b. $x - 2 = 5$ $\quad x - 2 + 2 = 5 + 2 \quad x = 7$

---

* When using algebra to solve problems stated in words, you must first be able to change the word expressions into algebraic expressions, that is, into the "language of algebra" (Reprinted with permission, Trivieri, 341). See pages 139–140 for The Language of Algebra Table.

5.0 EQUATIONS (continued)

RULE 2 The same number may be subtracted from both sides of an equation.

a. $3 + 8 = 11$ $\quad 3 + 8 - 3 = 11 - 3 \quad 8 = 8$

b. $x + 7 = 10$ $\quad x + 7 - 7 = 10 - 7 \quad x = 3$

RULE 3 Both sides of an equation may be multiplied by the same non-zero number.

a.

$$3 + 8 = 11$$
$$2 \times (3 + 8) = 2 \times 11$$
$$(2 \times 3) + (2 \times 8) = 22$$
$$6 + 16 = 22$$
$$22 = 22$$

b.

$$\frac{x}{3} = 7$$
$$3 \times \frac{x}{3} = 3 \times 7$$
$$x = 21$$

RULE 4 Both sides of an equation may be divided by the same nonzero number. Remember that you can never divide by zero!

a.

$$2 \times 5 = 10$$
$$\frac{2 \times 5}{2} = \frac{10}{2}$$
$$\frac{10}{2} = 5$$
$$5 = 5$$

b.

$$6x = 54$$
$$\frac{6x}{6} = \frac{54}{6}$$
$$x = \frac{54}{6}$$
$$x = 9$$

RULE 5 When an equation contains parentheses, we use the Distributive Law of Multiplication to remove the parentheses before solving for the unknown. The Distributive Law of Multiplication states that

$$a(b + c) = ab + ac$$

Example 2. Use the Distributive Law to remove the parentheses from $3(2x + 6) = 20$.

$$3(2x + 6) = 20$$
$$3(2x) + 3(6) = 20$$
$$6x + 18 = 20$$

Example 3. Solve $3x - 4 = 17$.

$$3x - 4 = 17$$

Add 4 to each side (Rule 1):

$$3x - 4 + 4 = 17 + 4$$
$$3x = 21$$

Divide both sides by 3 (Rule 4):

$$3x = 21$$
$$\frac{3x}{3} = \frac{21}{3}$$
$$x = 7$$

Let's check our solution to see if the value $x = 7$ satisfies the original equation.

Replace x with 7:

$$3x - 4 = 17$$
$$3(7) - 4 = 17$$
$$21 - 4 = 17$$
$$17 = 17 \quad \text{It checks!}$$

Example 4. Solve $28 + T = 39$.

$$28 + T = 39$$

Subtract 28 from each side (Rule 2):

$$28 - 28 + T = 39 - 28$$
$$T = 11$$

Example 5*. Solve $\frac{1}{2}y - 6 = 8$.

$$\frac{1}{2}y - 6 = 8$$

Add 6 to each side (Rule 1):

$$\frac{1}{2}y - 6 + 6 = 8 + 6$$
$$\frac{1}{2}y = 14$$

Multiply both sides by 2 (Rule 3):

$$2\left(\frac{1}{2}y\right) = 2(14)$$
$$y = 28$$

Example 6. Solve $w - \frac{2}{3} = \frac{4}{7}$.

$$w - \frac{2}{3} = \frac{4}{7}$$

Add $\frac{2}{3}$ to both sides (Rule 1):

$$w - \frac{2}{3} + \frac{2}{3} = \frac{4}{7} + \frac{2}{3}$$
$$w = \frac{4}{7} + \frac{2}{3}$$

$w = \frac{12 + 14}{21}$ The LCD for the unlike fractions is 21, so

$w = \frac{26}{21}$, or $1\frac{5}{21}$

* For help with solving fraction equations using a scientific calculator see the Hint on p. 56.

5.0 EQUATIONS (continued)

Alternative solution to Example 6.

Solve $W - \frac{2}{3} = \frac{4}{7}$

1. Find the LCD for 3 and 7. LCD = 21.

$21\left(W - \frac{2}{3}\right) = 21\left(\frac{4}{7}\right)$

2. Multiply both sides of the equation by 21, to remove the fractions.

$21W - 21\left(\frac{2}{3}\right) = 21\left(\frac{4}{7}\right)$

3. Use the Distributive Law on the left side.

$21W - 14 = 12$

$21W = 12 + 14$ Rule 1. (The addition rule)

$21W = 26$

$W = \frac{26}{21}$, or $1\frac{5}{21}$ Rule 4. (The division rule)

Example 7. Solve $10x + 7 = 3x + 49$.

$10x + 7 = 3x + 49$

Subtract 7 from each side (Rule 2):

$10x + 7 - 7 = 3x + 49 - 7$

$10x = 3x + 42$

Subtract $3x$ from both sides (Rule 2):

$10x - 3x = 3x - 3x + 42$

$7x = 42$

Divide both sides by 7 (Rule 4):

$\frac{7x}{7} = \frac{42}{7}$

$x = 6$

Example 8. Solve $8(2y + 4) = 112$.

$8(2y + 4) = 112$

Remove the parentheses using the Distributive Law (Rule 5):

$8(2y) + 8(4) = 112$

$16y + 32 = 112$

Subtract 32 from both sides (Rule 2):

$16y + 32 - 32 = 112 - 32$

$16y = 80$

Divide both sides by 16 (Rule 4):

$y = 5$

Example 9. Solve $61.393 = 8.41b$.

$61.393 = 8.41b$

Divide both sides by 8.41 (Rule 4):

$$\frac{61.393}{8.41} = \frac{8.41b}{8.41}$$

$$7.3 = b$$

That is, $b = 7.3$.

EXERCISE 5.0

Solve each of the following equations:

1. $12y + 6 = 30$

2. $\frac{x}{12} - 15 = 38$

3. $6x + 4(x + 7) = 148$

4. $\frac{x-5}{1.3} = 42.5$

5. $3x + 4 = 13$

6. $10p + 7 = 56 + 3p$

7. $\frac{3}{5}w = 9$

8. $2.31z = 122.199$

9. $4y - \frac{2}{5} = 2$

10. $m - 3\frac{1}{4} = 2\frac{1}{2}$

11. $\left(3\frac{1}{3}\right)x = 2\frac{1}{4}$

12. $4(3 - 7x) = -11$

13. $(4y - 3) + y = y + (5 - y)$

14. $\frac{2}{5}x + 3 = 4\left(\frac{7}{8} + \frac{1x}{12}\right)$

15. $0.38 + 1.1z = 0.6$

16. $\frac{0.4}{0.014} = \frac{0.08}{x}$

17. $4.3 = 0.3y - 7.34$

18. $\frac{4}{5}x = \frac{1}{10}x + \frac{2}{5}$

6.0 FORMULAS

Webster's Dictionary defines the word *formula* as "a set of algebraic symbols expressing a mathematical fact, principle, rule, etc. such as $I = PRT$." Many problems in business and in other areas involve the use of formulas. A formula is really an equation in which all the terms are represented by letters. If we know the values of all the terms except one, we can substitute those values for the letters of the formula. We can then solve the resulting equation.

Example 1. Given $I = PRT$. If $P = 4{,}000$, $R = 0.12$, and $T = 2$, find I.

$$I = PRT$$

Substitute the values of P, R, and T:

$$I = 4{,}000 \times 0.12 \times 2 = 960$$

When using formulas, you will need to meet two objectives. First, you must be able to evaluate formulas by substituting numbers for variables. Second, you must be able to solve a formula for a specific variable. Some examples of formulas are:

$I = PRT$	Interest = Principal × Rate × Time.
$D = RT$	Distance = Rate × Time.
$A = R \times B$	Amount of the Base = Rate × Base.
$S = P + PRT$	The amount to which a given principal will accumulate = Principal plus principal × Interest rate × Time.
$A = \frac{1}{2}bh$	Area of a triangle = One-half the length of the base × Length of the altitude.

There are as many different ways of writing a formula as there are letters in the formula.

Example 2. Write the formula $I = PRT$ four different ways (since the formula contains four variables).

(1) $I = PRT$

Divide both sides by PT.

(2) $\frac{I}{PT} = R$

Divide both sides of equation (1) by RT.

(3) $\frac{I}{RT} = P$

Divide both sides of equation (1) by PR.

(4) $\frac{I}{PR} = T$

Example 3. Write the formula $C = 25R$ to express R in terms of C.

$C = 25R$

Divide both sides of the formula by 25:

$\frac{C}{25} = \frac{25R}{25}$ $\qquad$ $\frac{C}{25} = R$ $\qquad$ $R = \frac{C}{25}$

Example 4. Given $ax + b = c$; $a \neq 0$. Express x in terms of a, b, and c.

$ax + b = c$

$ax + b - b = c - b$

$ax = c - b$

$x = \frac{c - b}{a}$

6.0 FORMULAS (continued)

Example 5. Given $I = PRT$, $I = \$540$, $R = 0.045$, and $P = \$6{,}000$, find T.

$$I = PRT$$

Divide both sides by PR:

$$\frac{1}{PR} = T$$

That is,

$$T = \frac{1}{PR}$$

Substitute the values of I, P, and R:

$$T = \frac{540}{(6,000)(0.045)} = \frac{540}{270} = 2 \text{ (years)}$$

[540] [÷] [(] [6000] [×] [0.045] [)] [=] 2

EXERCISE 6.0

1. Solve $2x + y = 6$ for y.

In each of the following formulas, substitute the given values and find the value of the unknown variable:

2. $D = RT$; $R = 55$ mph, $T = 3.5$ hours

3. $P = \frac{L + I}{T}$; $L = \$800$, $R = 12.4\%$, $T = 2$. Where $I = PRT$

$$\text{Monthly payment} = \frac{\text{Loan amount + Interest}}{\text{Number of months}}$$

4. Solve $I = PRT$ for T.

5. Solve $A = \frac{1}{2}bh$ for h.

6. Solve $E = \frac{Y + P}{Y}$ for P.

7. Solve $y = mxt + b$ for m.

8. Solve $\frac{T_1}{T_2} = \frac{V_1}{V_2}$ for V_2.

9. $I = PRT$; $P = \$9,000$, $R = 4.5\%$, $T = 2$ years. Find I.

10. $A = P + I$; $A = \$15,500$, $I = \$3,600$. Find P.

11. $C = \frac{300D + 7M}{100}$; $C = \$76.25$, $M = 875$. Find D.

12. $A = P(1 + RT)$; $P = \$14,600$, $R = 6.5\%$, $T = 6$ months. Find A. (***HINT:*** Express T in terms of years.)

P A R T

Practical Applications

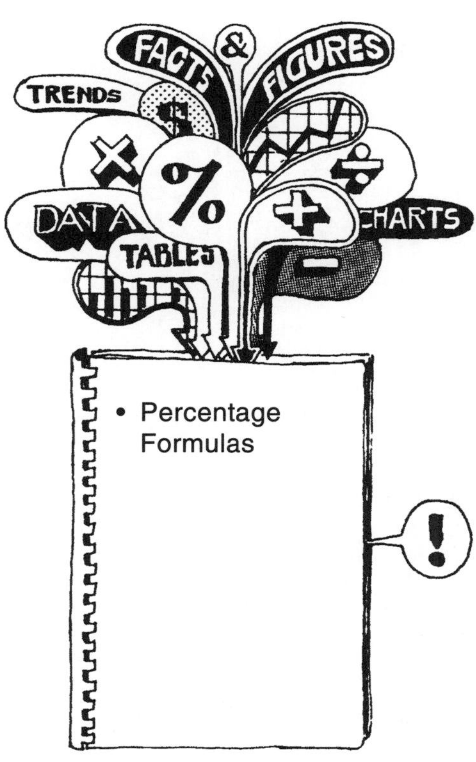

7.0 THE PERCENTAGE FORMULA

One of the most useful formulas in business is the percentage formula: $P = RB$, where P equals a percentage of the base, B, and R equals the rate (or percentage). Recall that if any two of the three variables are known, then the value of the remaining variable can be found.

Students often have difficulty determining which is the P, R, or B. Here is a simple way to figure it out: R is always given as a percentage; B is always the number that follows the word *of;* and P is what remains—P can also be thought of as coming before the word *is.*

For example, 10 percent of 40 is 4. Here, R is 10 (it comes before the word *percent*) B is 40 (it comes after the word *of*), and P is 4 (it comes after the word *is*).

Example 1. Identify R, B, and P:

a. 40 is what percent of 320?
↑ (40) P; ↑ (what) R; ↑ (320) B

b. 10 is 8% of what number?
↑ (10) P; ↑ (8%) R; ↑ (what) B

c. What is 75% of 200?
↑ (What) P; ↑ (75%) R; ↑ (200) B

7.1 Solving Problems with the Percentage Formula

The basic percentage formula can be discussed from two perspectives: with a visual geometric approach using a circle (see Figure 7.1) and with proportions.

Since the formula $P = R \times B$ has three variables, if we know any two of them we can find the remaining one.

The circle shown in Figure 7.1 may help you solve the percentage formula more easily. P is always in the half-circle. To find P, B, or R, simply shade the unknown segment you are solving for. If the remaining variables are horizontal, multiply them; if they are vertical, divide them.

7.0 THE PERCENTAGE FORMULA (continued)

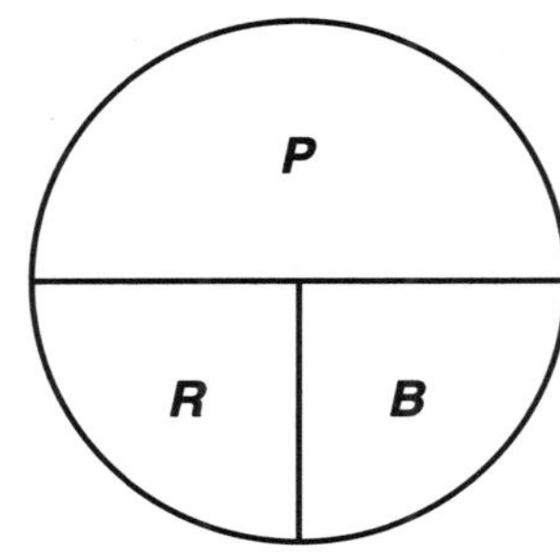

Figure 7.1 The $P = RB$ circle.

Example 2. Given R and B, find P.

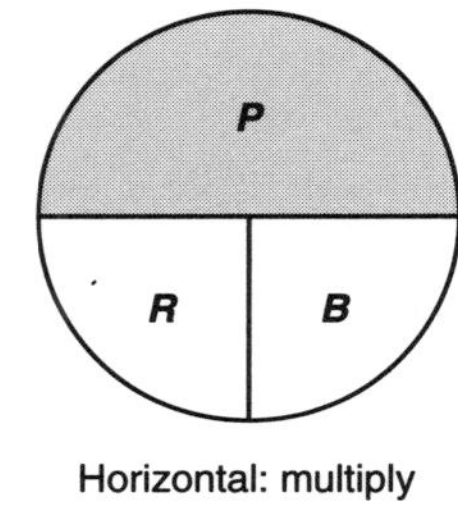

Example 3. Given P and B, find R.

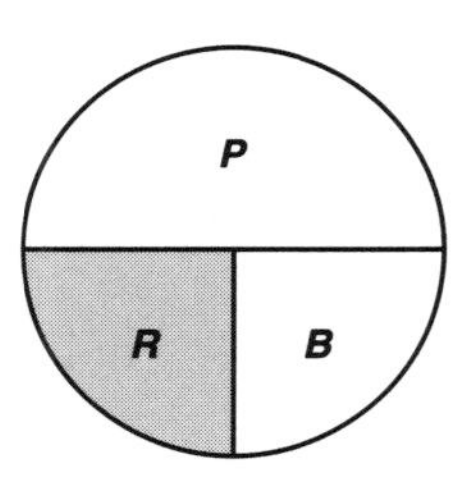

Example 4. Given P and R, find B.

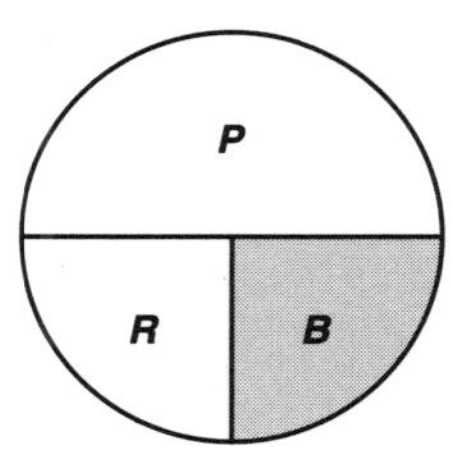

Once you know which form of the formula to use, you can substitute the given values for two of the terms to find the third, unknown term.

Example 5. What is 14% of 75.3?

$$P = RB$$
$$= (0.14)(75.3) = 10.542$$

Example 6. 10.542 is what percentage of 75.3?

$$R = \frac{P}{B}$$
$$= \frac{10.542}{75.3} = 0.14, \text{ or } 14\%$$

Example 7. 10.542 is 14% of what amount?

$$B = \frac{P}{R}$$
$$= \frac{10.542}{0.14} = 75.3$$

Example 8. Use a calculator to find 32.08% of 101.

$$P = RB$$
$$= (0.3208)(101)$$

Multiply using a calculator: [0.3208] [×] [101] [=] *32.4008*

or [101] [×] [32.08] [=] [2nd] [=] *32.4008*

or [32.08%] [2nd] [=] [×] [101] [=] *32.4008*

Note: The key sequence may be different for your calculator. Refer to your manual.

7.0 THE PERCENTAGE FORMULA (continued)

The second method we can use in working with the percentage formula is the proportion method. Before we use proportions, we need to understand what a ratio is. A *ratio* is a comparison of two quantities. A ratio is simply a fraction. Earlier in this text when we studied fractions, we could have called our fractions *ratios.* Thus, $\frac{1}{2}$, $\frac{7}{3}$, and $\frac{4}{5}$ are ratios.

A *proportion* is a comparison of ratios. For example, $\frac{1}{2} = \frac{5}{10}$ is a proportion. Since a proportion is also an equation, the rules for solving equations apply. Of all of the different mathematical concepts you will encounter in your study of mathematics, the concepts of ratio and proportion have perhaps the greatest number of everyday practical applications. Proportions are used in mixing ingredients, in comparison shopping, in solving problems using $P = R \times B$, and in many other applications.

We will now use proportions to solve problems based on the $P = RB$ formula. In using proportions, we always need to compare two ratios. The first ratio, the percentage ratio, is $\frac{R}{100}$. The second ratio is $\frac{P}{B}$. The proportion is: $\frac{R}{100} = \frac{P}{B}$, or $\frac{\text{Percent}}{100} = \frac{\text{Amount}}{\text{Base}}$. Some students find that $\frac{R}{100} = \frac{P}{B}$ is less clear than using the proportion $\frac{\%}{100} = \frac{\text{is}}{\text{of}}$.

Example 9. $\underbrace{49}_{P}$ $\underbrace{\text{is}}_{\text{equals}}$ what $\underbrace{\text{percentage}}_{R}$ $\underbrace{\text{of}}_{\text{multiplied by}}$ $\underbrace{102}_{B}$?

$$\frac{R}{100} = \frac{P}{B}, \quad \text{or} \quad \frac{\%}{100} = \frac{\text{is}}{\text{of}}$$

Example 10. 16 is 80% of what number?

$$\frac{R}{100} = \frac{P}{B}$$

Substitute the values of R and P:

$$\frac{80}{100} = \frac{16}{B}$$

$$80B = 16 \times 100$$

$$B = \frac{1,600}{80} = 20$$

Example 11. What is 1.06% of 500? P is the unknown. Substitute the values of R and B.

$$\frac{1.06}{100} = \frac{P}{500}$$

$$P = \frac{1.06 \times 500}{100} = \frac{530}{100} = 5.3$$

Example 12. The American College of Sports Medicine recommends the following formula to determine your level of intensity when you exercise, based on your age.

220 – (Your age) = ________, Your age-predicted maximum heart rate

Note: 220 is the maximum heart rate of an infant. You should train at approximately 65 to 85 percent of your age-predicted heart rate.

A 30-year-old person:

$$220 - 30 = 190$$
$$190 \times 0.65 = 124 \text{ beats/minute}$$
$$190 \times 0.85 = 162 \text{ beats/minute}$$

Thus, the target heart rate range should be between 124 and 162 beats/minute for this 30-year-old person.

7.0 THE PERCENTAGE FORMULA (continued)

EXERCISE 7.1

1. 49 is what percentage of 102?
2. 16 is 80% of what number?
3. What is 1.06% of 500?
4. What is $1\frac{1}{2}$% of 250?
5. 80% of 16.25 is what?
6. Find 31.187% of 97,580.
7. 3.7 is what percentage of 135?
8. What percentage of 40 is 1?
9. 125% of what is 48?
10. $66\frac{2}{3}$% of what is 9?
11. 5.19% of what is 103.8?
12. You can purchase a computer today for $4,500, which is 35% of the cost three years ago. What was the cost of the computer three years ago? Express your answer to the nearest whole dollar.
13. What is the target heart rate range for a person who is:
    a. 62 years old?
    b. 17 years old?

7.2 Commissions

A person's compensation is often paid on a commission basis, particularly if the job involves selling. A commission is a percentage of the total amount of sales. To find the commission earned, we multiply the amount of sales by the *rate of commission,* which is a percentage of the sales.

Commission = Rate of commission × Amount of sale

$$C = R \times A$$

Notice how the above formula is just like $P = RB$, but using different letters.

Example 1. Lorraine sells real estate and receives a commission of 5% of the sales price. What is Lorraine's commission on a house that sells for $125,700?

$$\begin{aligned} C &= R \times A \\ &= 0.05 \times \$125{,}700 = \$6{,}285 \end{aligned}$$

Example 2. Stephen works on a straight commission basis of 4% of his net sales. If Stephen's commission for last week was \$205, what was the amount of his net sales?

$$C = R \times A$$
$$205 = 0.04A$$
$$A = \frac{205}{0.04} = \$5,125$$

Example 3. Kim works at Friendly's Restaurant Equipment Company and receives a commission of 1% on the first \$1,000 of sales, 1.75% on the next \$200 in sales, and 2.1% on all sales over \$1,200.

If Kim's total net sales amounted to \$2,600, what was her commission?

$$\begin{aligned} C &= R \times A \\ &= (0.01)(\$1{,}000) + (0.0175)(\$200) + (0.021)(\$1{,}400) \\ &= \$10 + \$3.50 + 29.40 = \$42.90 \end{aligned}$$

EXERCISE 7.2

1. John sells textbooks worth a total of \$53,720. The publisher pays him an 11% commission on his sales. What was the amount of John's commission?
2. A computer salesperson received a commission of \$3,607.40 on sales of \$47,533. What is the rate of commission?
3. A salesperson has a commission rate of 4.7%. What volume of sales must she achieve to earn a commission of \$280?
4. Joey is paid a straight commission of 6% on net sales. Last month her gross sales totaled \$13,875, with returns totaling \$2,124. What was Joey's commission?
5. If Raoul receives a base salary of \$120 per week plus a commission of 8% of net sales, what is Raoul's earning if his gross sales for one week were \$3,459 with \$412 in returns?

7.0 THE PERCENTAGE FORMULA (continued)

6. Mark sells advertising space in a local magazine under a compensation plan of salary plus commission of 3.5% on net sales. Mark's salary is $185 and his net sales last week were $1,592. What was his income last week?

7. The Portsmouth Collection Agency provides a service for local businesses by collecting on delinquent accounts. An agent for the Portsmouth Collection Agency, Michele Croteau, collected $3,780. She was reimbursed at a rate of 25% for her services. She also received $41 for her expenses. After paying Michele's commission and expenses, how much did the Portsmouth Collection Agency receive?

8. The Century 35 Real Estate Agency's fee was $2,361.90. If the rate of commission was $6\frac{3}{4}$%, what was the selling price of the lot that the agency sold?

9. In December, John Croteau submitted orders totaling $21,538, with cancellations amounting to $3,675. John is paid on a graduated commission of 4.5% on the first $8,000 in net sales, 5.5% on the next $4,000, and 6.25% of net sales in excess of $12,000. What were John's earnings?

7.3 Percent Increase (Markup)

We encounter the concept of *percent increase* whenever a person is given a pay raise, the value of a house appreciates, the price of gasoline goes up, or the property tax on a home is raised.

The amount of increase is equal to the rate of increase multiplied by the original amount. In other words, it is once again $P = R \times B$.

Example 1. The price of gasoline last year was $1.09 per gallon. There has been a 40% increase in the price. What is the amount of increase?

$$\begin{aligned}\text{Amount of increase} &= \text{Rate of increase} \times \text{Original amount} \\ &= 0.40 \times \$1.09 = \$.44, \text{ or } 44 \text{ cents}\end{aligned}$$

Occasionally, we know the original amount and the new amount and wish to find the rate of increase.

Example 2. Last year the price of gasoline was \$1.09 per gallon. Today it is \$1.53 per gallon. What is the rate of increase?

$$\text{Rate of increase} = \frac{\text{Amount of increase}}{\text{Original amount}}$$

$$= \frac{\$.44}{\$1.09} = 0.4036, \text{ or approximately } 40\%$$

Example 3. The cost of a man's three-piece suit is \$350. The cost will increase by 12% in January. What will be the new purchase price of the suit?

First, we need to determine the amount of increase.

$P = R \times B$
$= .12 \times \$350 = \$42$

Then we must add this amount of increase to the original amount.

New purchase price = \$350 + \$42 = \$392

EXERCISE 7.3

1. The ABC Computer Company hired 250 new employees between July and December. At the beginning of the year, the total number of employees was 2,000. What was the percent increase in the number of employees?

2. After the Christmas holiday season Sam's weight increased from 167 pounds to 183 pounds. What is the percent increase in Sam's weight?

3. A share of common stock rose from $\$27\frac{1}{2}$ per share to $\$29\frac{5}{8}$ per share. Find the percent change in the stock value.

4. Deborah has \$737 in her savings account. She makes a deposit of \$53. What is the percent increase in her account?

5. A coffee table that costs \$119.22 sells for \$160.95. Find (a) the markup and (b) the rate of markup.

7.0 THE PERCENTAGE FORMULA (continued)

6. A video game cost $83 and was sold at a markup of 60 percent of the selling price. What is the selling price?

7. An item that sells for $180 has a markup of 40% of the selling price. What is the cost? (***Hint:*** Use the formula:

$$S = \frac{C}{1 - R(s)}$$

where S = selling price, C = the cost, and $R(s)$ = percentage of selling price.)

8. The annual snowfall along the New Hampshire seacoast was 34.5 inches in 1986 and 46 inches in 1987. What was the percent increase between 1986 and 1987?

9. A local jeweler sells for $18.04 a travel alarm clock that cost $12.95. What is the percent markup (to the nearest whole number) based on the cost?

10. The ABC Office Equipment store paid $229 for an electric typewriter. The store plans to mark up the cost by 40% of the selling price. What is the selling price?

11. If the Ford Motor Co. price hike of 2% increased the cost of a Taurus GL to $19,535, what was the previous price?

7.4 Percent Decrease (Markdown)

Whenever we purchase an item on sale we benefit from a percent decrease. Business managers are constantly facing changing numbers, such as variations in expenses, wage changes, or drops in sales.

The amount of decrease is equal to the rate of decrease multiplied by the original amount. Again, use our familiar equation $P = R \times B$ to determine amount of decrease.

Example 1. A new dress, which usually sells at \$160, is discounted at 20%. What is the amount of decrease?

$$\text{Amount of decrease} = \text{Rate of decrease} \times \text{Original amount}$$
$$= 0.20 \times \$160 = \$32$$

Example 2. Last week the price of gasoline decreased by 5%. If a gallon of gasoline sold for \$1.10 before the decrease, what was the amount of decrease?

$$P = R \times B$$
$$= 0.05 \times \$1.10$$
$$= \$0.06, \text{ or 6 cents}$$

Example 3. If the original price was \$1.09 and the new price was \$1.04, what is the rate of decrease?

First, we must find the amount of decrease.

$$\text{Amount of decrease} = \text{Original price} - \text{New price}$$
$$= \$1.09 - \$1.04 = \$0.05$$

Then we find the rate of decrease by applying the percentage formula.

$$\text{Rate of decrease} = \frac{\text{Amount of decrease}}{\text{Original amount}}$$
$$= \frac{\$0.05}{\$1.09}$$
$$= 0.0458$$
$$= 4.48\%, \text{ or } 5\% \text{ rounded to the nearest whole number}$$

7.0 THE PERCENTAGE FORMULA (continued)

EXERCISE 7.4

1. Your checking account shows a balance of $736. After writing several checks, your balance is $573.45. What is the percent decrease in your account?

2. After a strenuous weekend playing golf and tennis, Sam's weight dropped from 192 to 179 pounds. What was the percent decrease in Sam's weight?

3. The dividend for XYZ stock decreased from $13.50 per share to $11.85 per share. What was the rate of decrease?

4. What was the markdown percentage of net sales if the markdowns were $2,238 on sales of $23,560?

5. The local hardware store is having a 20%-off sale. An electric screwdriver is discounted $16. Find (a) the original price and (b) the sale price of the electric screwdriver.

6. What is the original price of a lawnmower that has been discounted 40% to $570?

7. A break-even point is the point at which revenue equals cost. A sofa that usually sells for $369.95 is advertised at $25 off the selling price. The cost of the sofa is $231.84 and there is an overhead of 40% of the cost. (a) Find the break-even point for the selling price of the sofa. (b) Does the advertised price result in a profit or a loss? How much?

8. Because of inclement weather, the number of people attending the last three games of the New England Patriots season decreased by 20% from the previous season. If there were an average of 83,750 people at the last three games of last year, on average how many were in attendance for the last three games this year?

7.5 Discount

Discount is the difference between the regular price and the sale price. Another way to consider this is that the sale price is the difference between the regular price and the discount. Advertisements frequently state discount as a percentage of the product's regular price.

Example 1. The Hampton Hardware store is selling its $32 heating lamp for 15% off the regular price. What is the discount?

$$\begin{aligned}\text{Discount} &= \text{Rate of discount} \times \text{Regular price}\\ &= 0.15 \times \$32 = \$4.80\end{aligned}$$

Example 2. A clothier is selling a sweater, regularly priced at $60, marked down to $45. (a) What is the discount? (b) What is the discount rate?

(a) $$\begin{aligned}\text{Discount} &= \text{Regular price} - \text{Sales price}\\ &= \$60 - \$45 = \$15\end{aligned}$$

(b) $$\begin{aligned}\text{Discount rate} &= \frac{\text{Discount}}{\text{Regular price}}\\ &= \frac{\$15}{\$60} = 0.25, \text{ or } 25\%\end{aligned}$$

EXERCISE 7.5

1. A snowblower that regularly sells for $600 is on sale for $75 off the regular price. What is the discount rate?

2. The marked price (regular price) of a computer is $1,525. What is the sale price if the rate of discount is 15%?

3. Many companies offer a small discount if you pay your bill promptly. John will get a 3% discount on his $537.38 bill if he pays the bill within 10 days. If John takes advantage of his discount, how much will he pay?

7.0 THE PERCENTAGE FORMULA (continued)

4. During an after-Christmas sale, a local furniture store is selling chairs at $86 less 20%. What is the total price a customer pays for a set of four chairs?

5. A wristwatch is on sale for $95 after a discount (markdown) of 45% off the regular price. What is the regular price?

7.6 Sales Tax

Most states collect a sales tax on selected products to raise revenue for government expenses and services. The tax rates vary from state to state, as do the types of products being taxed. Not only do states charge a sales tax, but so do cities, towns, and counties. A sales tax is also called a *personal property tax.* A sales tax is a percentage of the price of an item; that is,

Sales tax = Sales tax rate × Price of an item

This is another example of our now familiar percentage formula, $P = R \times B$.

Example 1. Mark has just purchased a new car for $11,750. A sales tax of 5% must be paid on his car. How much must he pay?

$$\begin{aligned}\text{Sales tax} &= \text{Sales tax rate} \times \text{Price of item}\\ &= 0.05 \times \$11{,}750 = \$587.50\end{aligned}$$

Example 2. What is the sales tax rate if the sales tax is $1.26 on an item priced at $42?

$$\begin{aligned}P &= R \times B\\ \$1.26 &= R \times \$42\\ R &= \frac{\$1.26}{\$42} = 0.03, \text{ or } 3\%\end{aligned}$$

EXERCISE 7.6

1. The price of an item is $120 and the tax rate is 2.5%. What is the amount of sales tax?

2. The purchase price of a sapphire ring is $549. You also have to pay a state sales tax of 6% and a city sales tax of 1.5%. What is the total cost of the ring?

3. Lorraine bought a new dress with a retail price of $195. The sales tax was $3\frac{1}{2}$%. She paid cash and received a 5% cash discount. What was her total cost?

4. Determine the sales tax rate if the sales tax is $14.20 on an item that sells for $495.

5. Roger has to pay a city tax of $3\frac{1}{2}$% and a county tax of $2\frac{3}{4}$% on his purchase of a new golf cart, which he bought for $850.99. How much tax did he pay?

6. Determine the sales tax rate for a garden cart that sells for $250 plus sales tax of $8.75.

7. Alice purchased three pairs of designer jeans for $41.50 per pair. She had to pay a delivery charge of $11.30 and a sales tax of 3.8% on her purchase. If Alice pays within 10 days, she gets an $8\frac{1}{2}$% discount. What is the total cost of the jeans if Alice pays within 10 days? (There is no discount allowed on delivery.)

8. A business had a day's receipts of $3,714, which included a 2% sales tax. How much were the sales?

9. Determine the sales tax rate on an item costing $63.50 if the sales tax was $2.54.

7.0 THE PERCENTAGE FORMULA (continued)

7.7 Property Tax

Our discussion of property tax will be limited to *real property tax.* Real property tax is paid on land and buildings, whereas personal property tax is paid on such items as clothing and automobiles, as discussed in the previous section.

Property tax is assessed using the formula:

Property tax = Tax rate × Assessed valuation

Does this look familiar? It's another variation of $P = R \times B$.

The assessed valuation is defined to be the rate of assessment multiplied by the fair market value. The tax rate is usually given in one of two ways, as a percent or as a dollar amount per $1,000.

Example 1. The property tax rate in Franklin is $18.75 per $1,000 of assessed value. How much tax must Steve pay if his property is assessed at $87,900?

We must first determine how many $1,000s there are in $87,900.

$$\frac{\$87,900}{\$1,000} = 87.9$$

Next we must multiply 87.9 by the tax rate per $1,000.

87.9 × $18.75 = $1,648.13

This is the amount of the annual property tax Steve must pay.

Example 2. If the property tax rate is 3.25% in the town of Rye, what is the property tax on a house having an assessed valuation of $52,400?

Property tax = Tax rate × Assessed valuation
= 0.0325 × $52,400 = $1,703

EXERCISE 7.7

1. An office condominium building has been assessed at $760,000 in a city whose tax rate is $12.50 per $1,000 of assessed valuation. Find the property tax.

2. If the assessed value of a house is $34,500 and the tax rate is $16.50 per $1,000, what is the amount of property tax to be paid?

3. How much property tax must be paid on property having an assessed value of $123,200 if the tax rate is 2.04%?

4. What is the property tax rate for a town whose total budget is $3,719,304 and whose total assessed value is $79,570,000?

5. The tax rate in New Ulm is $.0515 per $1.00 of assessed valuation. How much tax must the Hansons pay on two pieces of real estate valued at $54,000 and $31,000, if these two pieces are assessed at 65% of their value?

6. The property tax on a building is $1,407.45. If the tax rate is 1.36%, find the assessed value, correct to the nearest dollar.

7. Determine the amount of property tax on property whose value is $244,700, assessed at 71% of its fair market value. The tax rate is 34 mills. (1 mill = 0.001 of a dollar.)

8. Determine the amount of property tax on property whose assessed valuation is $19,950 at a tax rate of 23.7 mills per dollar.

7.8 Simple and Compound Interest

If we borrow money from a bank, we pay *interest* for the use of the loan. For example, if the interest rate is 9%, we have to pay back the amount we borrowed plus 9% of the amount. Conversely, when you deposit money into a savings account, the bank will pay you interest for the use of your money. Suppose a bank will you give 5% simple interest on the money you deposit in your account. If you place a sum of money in your account and leave it there for one year, you will then have the original sum plus 5% in your account.

7.0 THE PERCENTAGE FORMULA (continued)

The interest earned on the original sum is called *simple interest.* The interest we earn can be added to the original sum and included in subsequent calculations of interest. The interest calculated in this way is called *compound interest.*

Three factors determine the amount of simple interest, whether you borrow money or save money. These three factors are principal, rate of interest, and time. The *principal,* denoted by P, is the amount of money borrowed or saved. The *rate* of interest, denoted by R, is a percentage per period of time, usually a year. The *time,* denoted by T, is expressed in years (or a fraction of a year).

The simple interest formula is:

$$I = PRT$$

The compound interest formula is:

$$A = P\left(1 + \frac{r}{n}\right)^{nt}$$

A is the amount accumulated
P is the original principal
r is the interest rate
n is the number of compounding periods
t is the time in years

As stated earlier compound interest is determined by simply adding interest earned to the original principal, then calculating the interest on this new amount, etc. for several compounding periods.

Banks and other savings institutions use compound interest tables to determine accumulated amounts rather than "number crunching" each period.

As we prepare for our retirement, it is essential that we save in accounts that use compounding such as Tax Sheltered Annuities or CD's (Certificates of Deposit) since compounding will produce a larger amount of interest.

Example 1. Find the simple interest earned on a deposit of $1,110 at 6.5% for a period of one year.

$I = PRT$

P = $1,110
R = 6.5%, or 0.065
T = 1

I = ($1,110)(0.065)(1)
= $72.15

Example 2. Find the simple interest owed on $650 borrowed at $4\frac{1}{4}$% for 9 months. In this problem we must convert 9 months to an equivalent part of one year before we use our formula.

$$9 \text{ months} = \frac{9}{12} \text{ year} = \frac{3}{4} \text{ year} = 0.75 \text{ year}$$

$I = PRT$
= ($650)(0.0425)(0.75) = $20.72

If the time is expressed in days, we must convert it to an equivalent part of one year. There are two ways of doing this. With the *exact method,* the time in years is equal to the number of days divided by 365. With the *ordinary method* (also referred to as the banker's method), the time in years equals the number of days divided by 360. We will use the ordinary method in this text.

Example 3. Find the simple interest owed on $980 at 5.5% for 90 days.

$$90 \text{ days} = \frac{90}{360} \text{ year} = \frac{1}{4} \text{ year} = 0.25 \text{ year}$$

$I = PRT$
= ($980)(0.055)(0.25) = $13.48

7.0 THE PERCENTAGE FORMULA (continued)

Example 4. The interest on a 45-day loan of $7,600 is $52.25. Find the simple interest rate.

$$I = PRT$$

Therefore,

$$\frac{I}{PT} = R$$

That is,

$$R = \frac{I}{PT}$$

$$= \frac{\$52.25}{(\$7,600)(\frac{45}{360})} = \frac{\$52.25}{(\$7,600)(\frac{1}{8})} = \frac{\$52.25}{\$950} = 0.055, \text{ or } 5\tfrac{1}{2}\%$$

Here is a summary of the time conversions:

Time in months: $T = \dfrac{\text{Time in months}}{12}$ year

Time in days (ordinary method): $T = \dfrac{\text{Time in days}}{360}$ year

Certain problems involving simple interest require us to calculate the time before we can use $I = PRT$.

Example 5. How much simple interest will be earned on a deposit of \$7,000 at 8%, if the money is deposited on July 25 and is withdrawn on September 8?

We must first determine the amount of time, that is, the total number of days.

Number of days in July:	31
Starting July date:	25
Number of July days to be counted (31 – 25):	6
Number of August days to be counted:	31
Number of September days to be counted:	8
Total number of days (6 + 31 + 8):	45

$$\begin{aligned} I &= PRT \\ &= (\$7{,}000)(0.08)\left(\tfrac{45}{360}\right) \\ &= (\$7{,}000)(0.08)(0.125) \\ &= \$70 \end{aligned}$$

The *amount is* defined as the sum of the principal and the interest.

To determine the amount, we must first find the interest, then add it to the principal.

Example 6.

$$\begin{aligned} A &= P + I \\ &= \$780 + \$38.50 = \$818.50 \end{aligned}$$

Example 7. Determine the total amount of a loan of \$600 at $4\frac{3}{4}$% for half a year.

$$\begin{aligned} I &= PRT \\ &= (\$600)(0.0475)\left(\tfrac{1}{2}\right) = \$14.25 \end{aligned}$$

Then find A.

$$\begin{aligned} A &= P + I \\ &= \$600 + \$14.25 = \$614.25 \end{aligned}$$

7.0 THE PERCENTAGE FORMULA (continued)

Example 8. What amount of money will be needed on December 11 to repay a loan taken on September 27 for \$4,800 at the simple interest rate of 10.5%? First, we need to determine the number of days.

September days:	3
October days:	31
November days:	30
December days:	11
	75

Second, we need to determine the interest.

$$
\begin{aligned}
I &= PRT \\
&= (\$4{,}800)(0.105)(\tfrac{75}{360}) = \$105
\end{aligned}
$$

Third, we need to determine the amount.

$$
\begin{aligned}
A &= P + I \\
&= \$4{,}800 + \$105 = \$4{,}905
\end{aligned}
$$

Example 9. Comparing simple interest and compound interest.

Bob deposited \$15,000 for three years at 6% simple interest in the Citizens Bank.

Using simple interest Bob would have earned \$2,700.

$$
\begin{aligned}
I &= PRT \\
&= \$15{,}000(0.06)(3) = \$2{,}700
\end{aligned}
$$

Using compound interest for \$15,000 for three years at 6% compound annually Bob would have earned \$2,865.24.

1st year	$I = \$15{,}000(0.06)(1) = \$900$
2nd year	$I = \$15{,}900(0.06)(1) = \$954$
3rd year	$I = \$16{,}854(0.06)(1) = \$1{,}011.24$

The total intest earned was \$900 + \$954 + \$1,011.24 = \$2,865.24. Bob earned \$165.24 more in the compound interest account than in the simple interest account.

$\$2{,}865.24 - \$2{,}700 = \$165.24$

The previous calculation using the compound interest formula is shown below:

$$A = P\left(1 + \frac{r}{n}\right)^{nt}$$

$$= \$15,000\left(1 + \frac{0.06}{1}\right)^{(1)(3)}$$

$$= \$15,000(1.06)^3 = \$15,000(1.191016) = \$17,865.24$$

Thus, \$17,865.24 – \$15,000 = \$2,865.24.

HINT: Remember to subtract your principal from the accumulated amount to find the interest.

[\$15,000] [×] [1.06] [y^x] [3] [=] → *\$17,865.24**

Example 10. Below is an interesting example to show the power of compounding and "the cost of waiting."

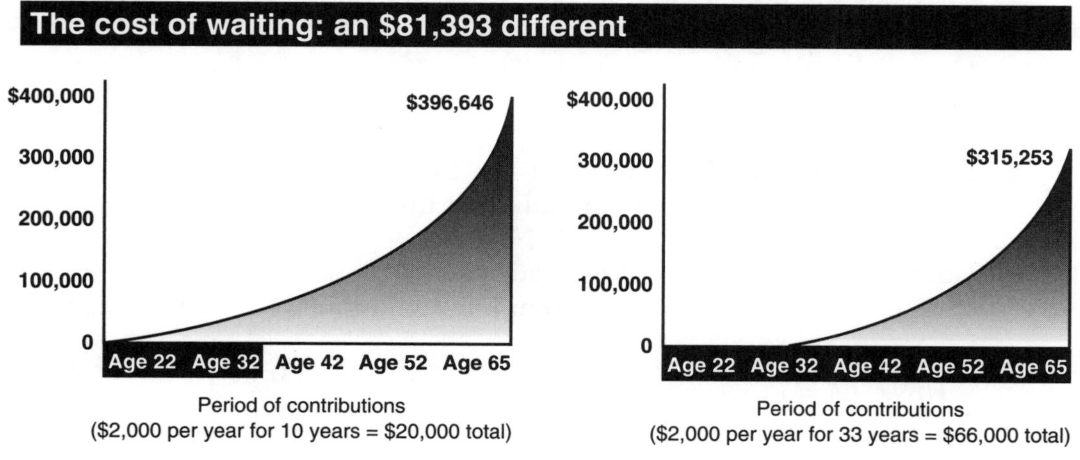

Charts reprinted by permission of MFS Fund Distributors, Inc.

* Note calculator key strokes.

7.0 THE PERCENTAGE FORMULA (continued)

EXERCISE 7.8

1. Find I if P = \$550, R = 8%, and T = 6 months.

2. What is the simple interest charged on a loan of \$450 at $9\frac{3}{4}$% if the loan is borrowed on May 18 and is to be repaid on August 6?

3. Find R if P = \$450, I = \$20.25, and T = 6 months.

4. What is the simple interest due on a loan of \$10,500 borrowed from a bank for 18 months at an annual interest rate of $7\frac{1}{2}$%?

5. Recall that $A = P + I$ (amount equals principal plus interest). Since $I = PRT$, $A = P + PRT$, or $A = P(1 + RT)$. Using the formula $A = P(1 + RT)$, what investment at 12% simple interest would have a maturity value of \$500 in 18 months? (***HINT:*** Solve the formula for P in terms of A, R, and T.)

6. Find the maturity date of a six-month note dated August 12, 1990.

7. How much interest is charged for a month if there is a balance of \$450 and the interest rate is 18% a year on the unpaid balance?

8. Find the compound interest on \$500 at 5% compounded annually for two years.

9. Find the compound amount and the compound interest on \$3,000 at $4\frac{1}{2}$% compounded semiannually for three years.

10. How large a desposit must be made to give an accumulated amount of \$1,094.99 if the rate is 4% compounded annually for five years?

    $$HINT\text{:}\ A = P\left(1 + \frac{r}{n}\right)^{nt} \quad or \quad \$1,094.99 = P\left(1 + \frac{0.04}{1}\right)^{1(5)}$$

    This is known as finding *present value.*

11. What is the compound interest on \$4,000 at 4% compounded monthly for one year?

12. John believes he will need $5,000 in four years to tour France. How much must be invested today at 8% compounded quarterly to have $5,000 in 4 years? Recall that

$$\text{Present value} = \frac{\text{Maturity value}}{\text{1 + Interest rate expressed as a decimal}}$$

7.9 Installment Loans

Installment loans are frequently used to finance the cost of items such as furniture, large appliances, and automobiles. Consumers also use credit cards to purchase retail items, thereby having the use of the item before it is fully paid. The consumer then pays for the product in equal installments; this is another type of installment loan. The disadvantage of installment payments to the consumer is that there is an additional expense. Imagine that you wish to buy a TV whose cost is $200. If you give a down payment of $50 and pay nine monthly payments of $20, you will end up paying $230 for the TV.

The *amount* financed is equal to the cash price minus the down payment.

The *finance charge* is equal to the amount financed times the interest rate times the time. In other words, it is $I = PRT$, dressed in new clothing. The rate in $I = PRT$ is called the *annual percentage rate.*

The *total of the installment payments* is the amount financed plus the finance charge.

The *monthly payment* is equal to the total of the installment payments divided by the number of monthly payments.

Example 1. Mark borrowed $450 from a friend. The money was paid back in 20 monthly payments of $28.20. How much was Mark's finance charge?

20 monthly payments × $28.20 = $564
$564 − $450 = $114

7.0 THE PERCENTAGE FORMULA (continued)

Example 2. A snowblower is priced at \$900 cash or \$90 down and 10 monthly payments. The finance charge is $12\frac{1}{2}\%$ of the unpaid balance. Find the amount of each monthly payment.

Unpaid balance:	\$900 − \$90 = \$810
Finance charge:	\$810 × 0.125 = \$101.25
Monthly payment:	(\$810 + \$101.25) ÷ 10 = \$91.13

Occasionally, consumers will pay off a loan early. Should you pay off a loan early, you will be entitled to receive back some of the prepaid interest. The lender will determine the amount of your interest rebate by using a technique known as the *Sum of the Digits method.*

To determine the amount of your rebate of interest using the Sum of the Digits method, you multiply the interest charged by the *rebate fraction.* The rebate fraction has a numerator equal to the sum of the digits of the remaining payments, and a denominator equal to the sum of the digits of the total number of payments.

Example 3. Salim has a 12-month loan, which he pays off in 9 months. What is the rebate fraction?

$$\text{Rebate fraction} = \frac{\text{Sum of the digits of the remaining payments}}{\text{Sum of the digits of the total payments}}$$

$$= \frac{1+2+3}{1+2+3+\ldots+11+12} = \frac{6}{78} = \frac{1}{13}$$

The summing of digits can be cumbersome, especially when there are a large number of digits to be added. Using the summation formula below can save us time.

$$\text{Sum} = N\frac{(N+1)}{2}, \text{ where } N \text{ is the number of payments.}$$

Example 4. Find the rebate fraction for Salim's loan (Example 3) using the summation formula.

The numerator consisted of three remaining payments; thus, $N = 3$.

$$\text{Sum of } 1 + 2 + 3 = \frac{3(3+1)}{2} = 6$$

The denominator consisted of twelve payments; thus, $N = 12$.

$$\text{Sum of } 1 + 2 + 3 + \ldots + 12 = \frac{12(12+1)}{2} = 78$$

So the rebate fraction $= \dfrac{6}{78}$.

Notice that the sum of the digits of the total payments is 78 when there are 12 payments. Since this is often the case, the Sum of the Digits method is also known as the Rule of 78ths. When there are 12 payments, the denominator of the rebate fraction is 78.

Example 5. A 12-month installment loan with \$55 payments and an interest charge of \$40 was paid in full at the end of 8 months. How much was the final payment?

STEP 1 Find the rebate fraction.

$$\text{Numerator: } \frac{4(4+1)}{2} = 10$$

Denominator: 78. The rebate fraction is $\dfrac{10}{78}$, or $\dfrac{5}{39}$.

STEP 2 Find the rebate.

$$\begin{aligned}\text{Rebate} &= \text{Rebate fraction} \times \text{Interest charged} \\ &= \frac{10}{78} \times \$40 = \$5.13\end{aligned}$$

STEP 3 Find the amount still owed.

$$\$55 \times 4 \text{ payments} = \$220$$

7.0 THE PERCENTAGE FORMULA (continued)

STEP 4 Find the final payment.

Final payment = Amount still owed – Interest rebate
= $220 – $5.13 = $214.87

EXERCISE 7.9

1. Steve and Elizabeth recently bought new living room furniture on an installment plan of 18 monthly payments of $60 each, with a down payment of $50. If they had paid cash they would have paid $1,000. How much in addition did they pay for buying on the installment plan?

2. Brigitte has just purchased a new stereo system on sale for $1,450. She bought it on the installment plan. She paid a down payment of $250 and financed the unpaid balance over 9 months at 10.5%. What is her monthly payment?

3. A charge of $275 was made August 15 on a credit card. The billing date was September 1; the due date is 30 days after the billing date. If the bill was paid on September 17, find the finance charge.

4. The credit card company in problem 3 charged a monthly finance charge of 1.2% on the unpaid balance. What would the balance on the $275 purchase be on October 2?

5. A hospital bill of $735 was paid for with $75 down and $60 a month for 12 months. What was the finance charge?

6. Simple interest is called *add-on* interest. Eugene recently bought a new car costing $12,500 on an installment plan. He made a down payment of 25% and will pay 10.25% simple add-on interest on the unpaid balance for three years. What is the amount financed?

7. Determine (a) the total interest paid and (b) the total installment price in problem 6.

8. The Lobster Trap Restaurant accepts VISA and MasterCard. Both VISA and MasterCard have a service charge of 5% on credit card purchases. If the Lobster Trap Restaurant had monthly VISA card sales of $35,700 and monthly MasterCard sales of $18,250, how much was paid (a) to VISA and (b) to MasterCard? The net credit card sales equals the amount remaining after subtracting the service charge. (c) Find the net credit card sales of the Lobster Trap Restaurant.

9. A loan is being paid in 12 equal monthly payments. At the end of the 6th month the loan is completely paid. What fractional part of the total interest need not be paid?

10. Lisa bought a new pair of skis and ski poles for $1,380. She made a down payment of $200 and agreed to pay the balance over two years at 10%. If she was able to pay off her loan in 12 months, how much was the pay-off amount?

PART

Graphs and Statistics

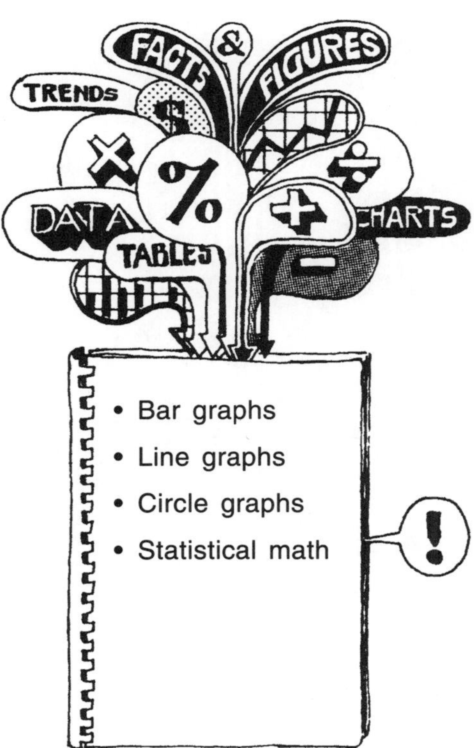

8.0 BAR GRAPHS

The following pages will show how the same statistical information can be presented using bar graphs, line graphs, and circle graphs using Mark's average monthly expenses as a common example. It should be noted, however, that one type of graph may be better suited to present your data than another. If you wish to show a trend, a line graph is the best choice. If you wish to compare related values, the bar graphs are best, and if you want to show how a whole quantity is being divided use circle graphs.

The percentage formula you studied earlier in Section 7 is often used to solve problems involving graphs.

Bar graphs have a horizontal axis and a vertical axis (see Figure 8.1). The two axes are labeled with data, enabling you to answer questions by reading the graph. Usually the graph represents approximate numbers rather than exact numbers. Each bar graph has a title, specifying what type of information is being shown.

Bar graphs can have vertical bars, as in Figure 8.1, or horizontal bars, as in Figure 8.2.

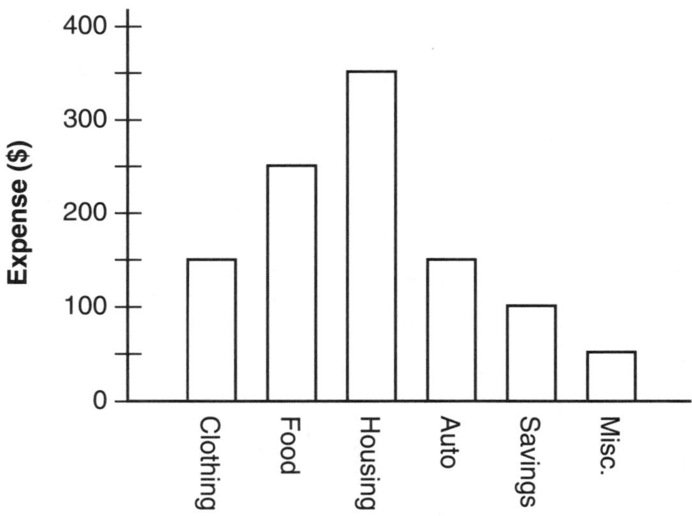

Figure 8.1 Bar graph

8.0 BAR GRAPHS (continued)

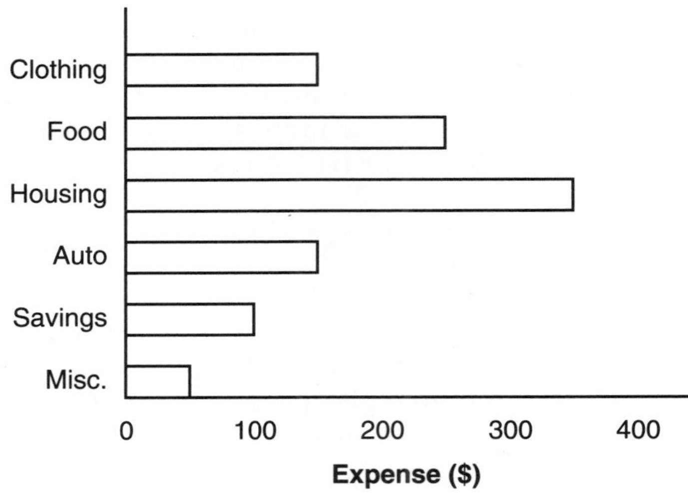

Figure 8.2 Horizontal bar graph

A *histogram* is a special type of bar graph. A bar graph is similar to a histogram, except that the bars are separated by space.

Example:

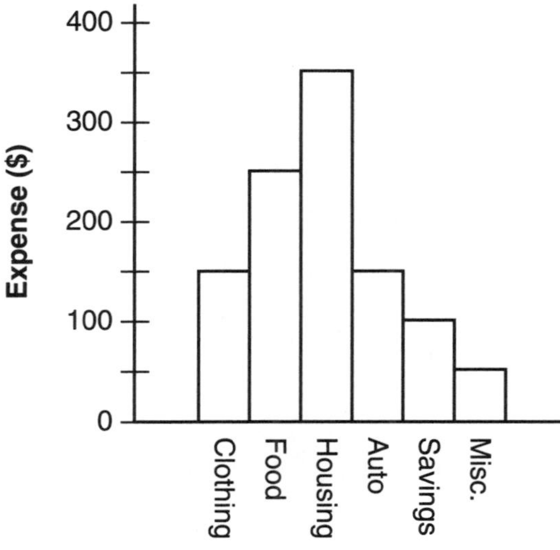

Figure 8.1 Histogram

A double bar graph can be used to compare two sets of data. For example, Mark's average monthly expenses for two successive years are compared in Figure 8.3.

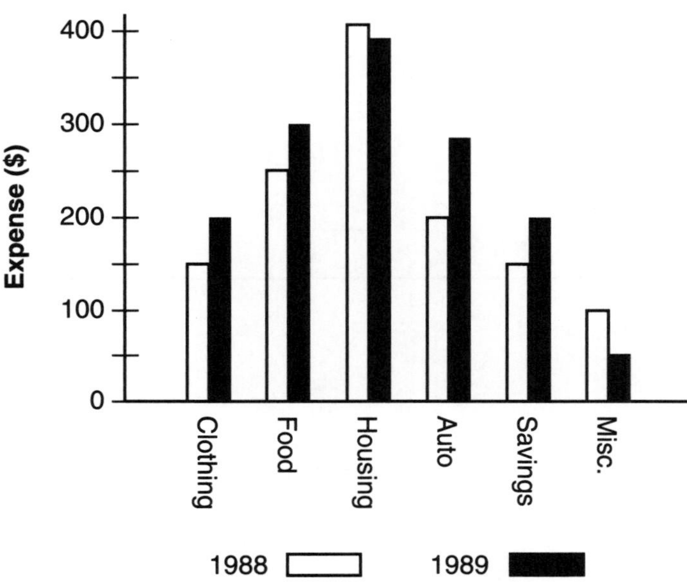

Figure 8.3 Double bar graph

8.0 BAR GRAPHS (continued)

EXERCISE 8.0

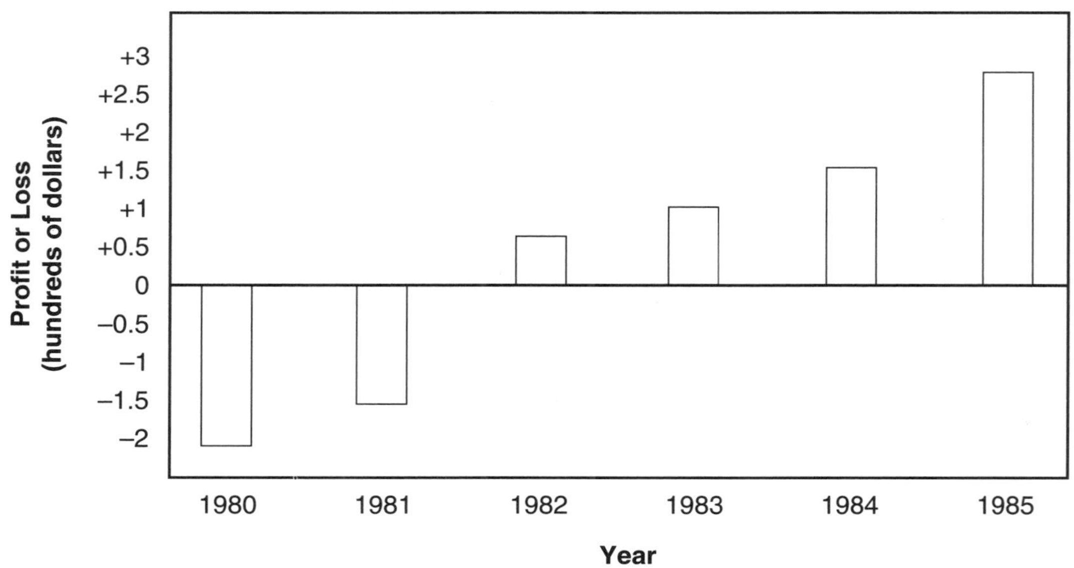

Use the above graph to answer questions 1–4:

1. During which year did the herb farm earn the most money?

2. Which year showed the greatest loss?

3. What was the percent increase in profits from 1982 to 1984?

4. Find the difference between the 1985 sales and the 1981 sales.

5. The January through June sales of Troy Clothiers were as follows: Jan., $15,000; Feb., $11,000; Mar., $12,500; Apr., $14,000; May, $18,500; June, $16,500. Draw a horizontal bar graph to represent this information.

6. Big Mike's fast food restaurant reported the following sales during the years 1985–1989.

Year	Plain Hamburger	Cheeseburger
1985	$5,000	$6,500
1986	$5,500	$7,500
1987	$6,200	$9,100
1988	$7,300	$10,300
1989	$8,000	$12,500

Construct a double bar graph showing hamburger sales and cheeseburger sales.

7. The Beau Brummel Haberdashery listed the following February sales: men's suits, $9,500; men's shoes, $2,700; men's shirts and accessories, $11,000. These were the total sales, including cash sales and credit sales. The cash sales were $7,500 for suits, $1,500 for shoes, and $9,000 for shirts and accessories. Prepare a bar graph showing cash sales, credit sales, and total sales for each of the three departments.

Use the following graph to answer questions 8–10.

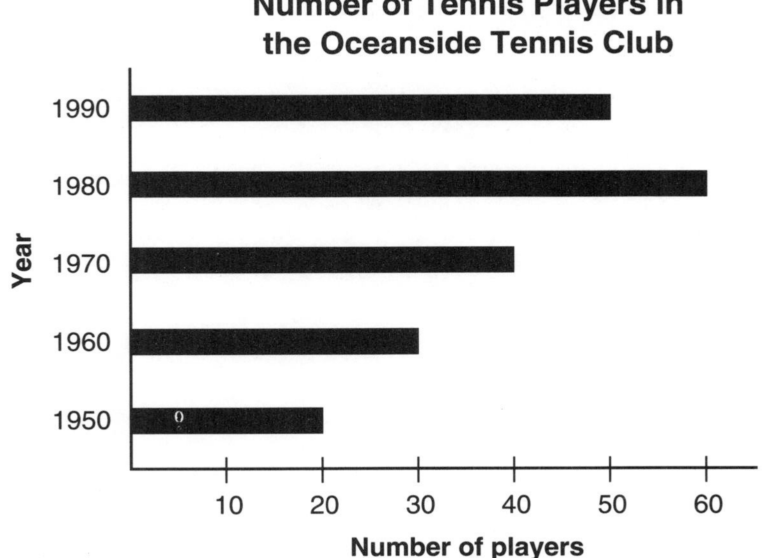

8.0 BAR GRAPHS (continued)

8. Write a ratio comparing the number of tennis players in 1950 to the number in 1990.

9. In what 10-year period did the club membership increase the most?

10. Based on the graph, would you expect an increase or decrease in club membership by the year 2000?

9.0 LINE GRAPHS

Line graphs are similar to bar graphs, but only the tops of the bars are marked. These points are then joined with a line. See Figure 9.1.

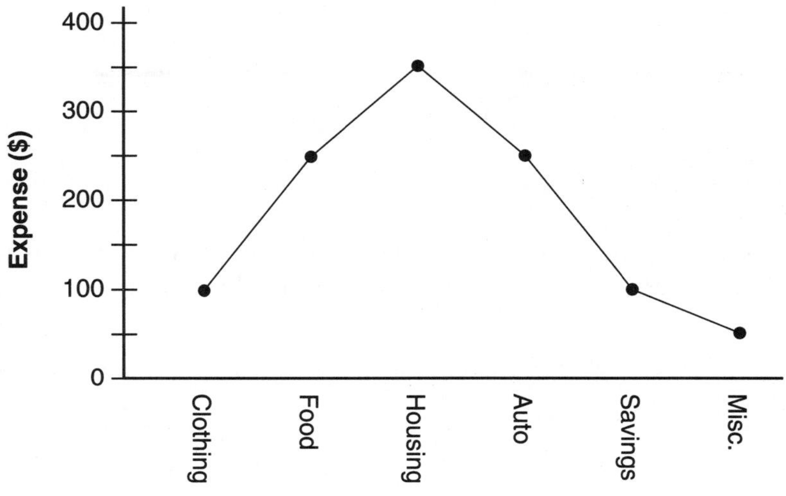

Figure 9.1 Line graph

Example 1. The Arc College Publishing Company had monthly profits as shown in the line graph in Figure 9.2.

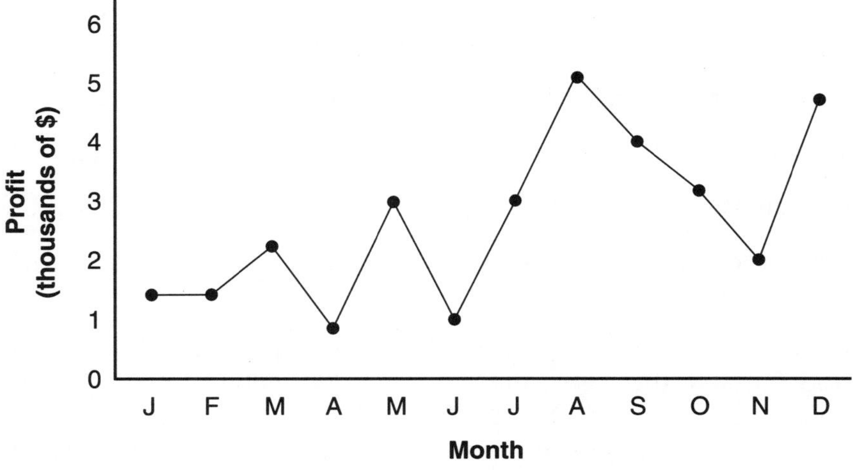

Figure 9.2 Line graph

9.0 LINE GRAPHS (continued)

a.	Which month had the greatest profit?	August
b.	Find the company's profit for October.	$3,000
c.	During which month was the company's profit the lowest?	April
d.	Find the company's profit for August.	$5,500

EXERCISE 9.0

Gender turnout, voter gap

In every presidential election since 1964, women have voted in greater numbers than men. Total number who reported voting:

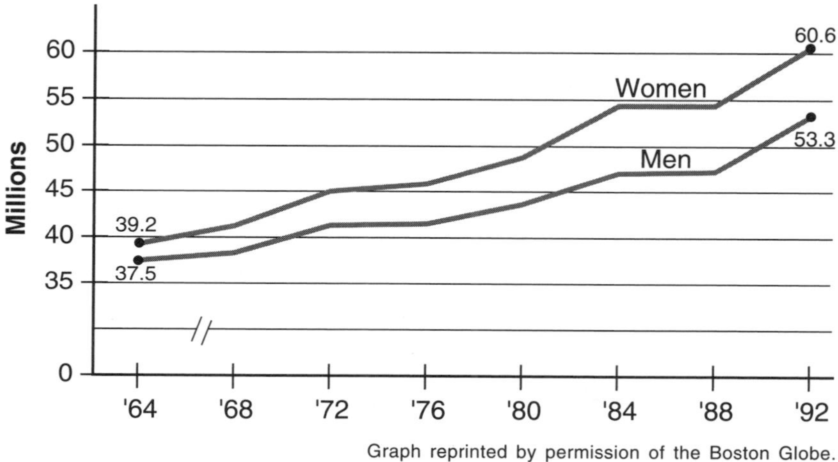

Graph reprinted by permission of the Boston Globe.

Use the above graph to answer questions 1–4.

1. In what year did 45 million women vote?
2. What was the percent increase in women voters from 1972 to 1984?
3. Approximately how many men voters were there in 1990?
4. What is the difference in percent increase between women and men voters between 1964 to 1992?
5. Draw a line graph to represent the sales of Troy Clothiers for the period January through June. Jan., $15,000; Feb., $11,000; March $12,500; April, $14,000; May, $18,500; June, $16,500. (Compare this graph with the bar graph you drew for problem 5 of Exercise 8.0.)

10.0 CIRCLE GRAPHS

You may recall from high school geometry that a circle contains 360°. When we construct a circle graph, we represent percentages by sectors of a circle (see Figure 10.1). If Mark spends 15% of his income on clothing, then the "Clothing" sector of the circle contains

$$360° \times 0.15 = 54°$$

Similarly, if Mark spends 26% of his income on food, then the "Food" sector of the circle contains

$$360° \times 0.26 = 94°$$

A circle graph is also known as a pie graph, because the sectors look like slices of a pie.

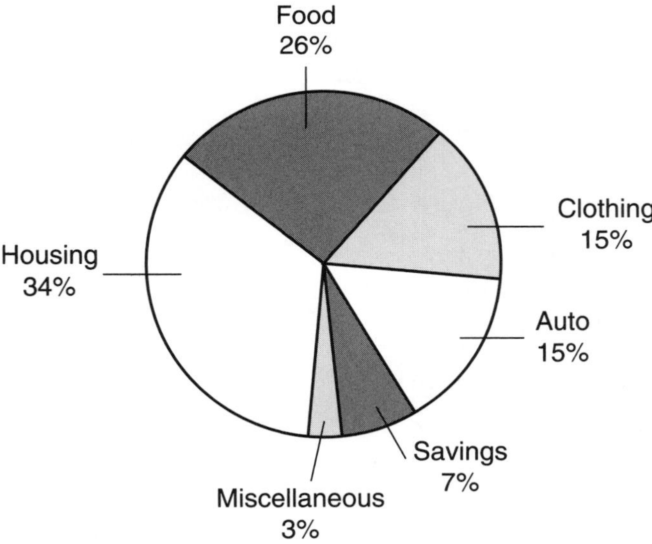

Figure 10.1 Circle graph (pie graph)

A personal computer is an excellent tool for constructing circle graphs. If you do not have access to a PC, you will need a compass, a ruler, and a protractor to construct circle graphs.

10.0 CIRCLE GRAPHS (continued)

Example 1. The Holmes Real Estate Company has an annual budget of $275,000. The circle graph in Figure 10.2 shows the percentage of the budget that is allocated to each item.

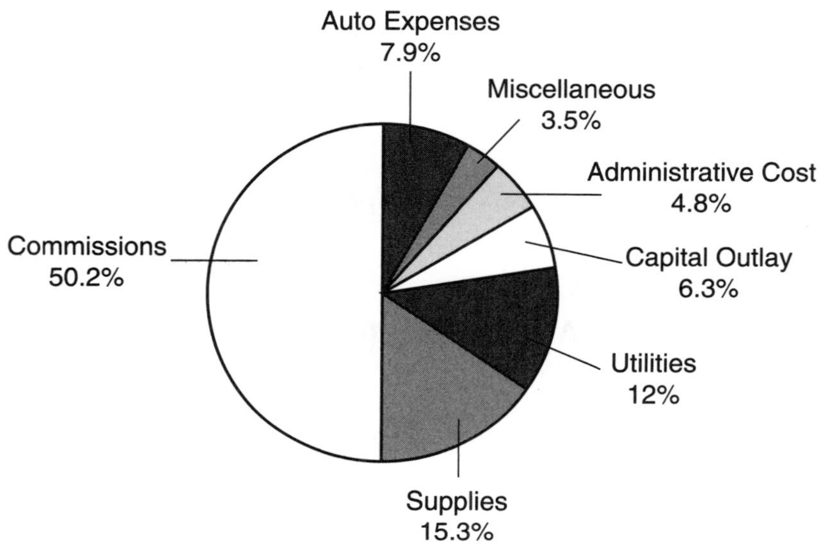

Figure 10.2 Circle graph

a. How much money is budgeted for utilities?
12% of $275,000 = $33,000

b. How much money is budgeted for auto expenses?
7.9% of $275,000 = $21,725.00

c. What percentage of the money is budgeted for supplies and utilities?
15.3% + 12% = 27.3%

d. What percentage of the money is budgeted for commissions and administrative costs?
50.2% + 4.8% = 55.0%

EXERCISE 10.0

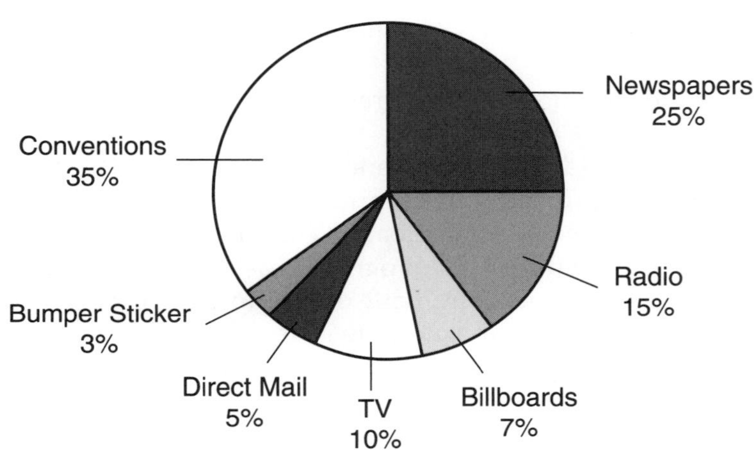

The Pennyroyal Herb Farms Advertising Budget for 1989 was $120,000. Use the circle graph above to answer questions 1–3.

1. What is the dollar amount budgeted for billboards?

2. How much was budgeted for newspapers and radio?

3. What does the budget of $120,000 represent in terms of percent?

4. The revenues of the Pennyroyal Herb Farm were distributed as follows: herbal wreaths, 13%; garden statuary, 24%; fresh-cut herbs, 27%; small plants, 36%. Draw a circle graph to represent this information.

5. Prepare a circle graph to illustrate the percentage of A, B, and C students at New Paul College.

A students	4,000
B students	5,600
C students	6,400

11.0 STATISTICAL MATH

On page 19 we examined the concept of an average. This average is also called the *arithmetic mean.* Two other kinds of averages are used in statistics, the *median* and the *mode.*

A *median* is the middle vaue in a set of values that are arranged in order from smallest to largest, or conversly. The median is the middle value if we have an odd number of values, and the median is the average of the two middle terms if we have an even number of values.

A *mode* is the value that occurs most frequently in a group of values.

The *range* of a set of data is the difference between the largest and smallest numbers. A small range means that the numbers are similar and a large range means that the numbers vary greatly. The range of a set of data can be greatly distorted by a single value, suggesting a larger spread of data than is actually the case. A better measurement of the spread of all the values from a central point in the distribution is known as *standard deviation.* Standard deviation is the measure of how much the data differ from the mean.

Example. Find the standard deviation of the following:

29, 20, 35, 27, 53, 28

STEP 1 Find the mean.

$$\frac{29 + 20 + 35 + 27 + 53 + 28}{6} = 32$$

STEP 2 Subtract the mean from each element of the data.

$$\left.\begin{array}{l} 53 - 32 = +21 \\ 35 - 32 = +3 \end{array}\right] +24 \quad \text{deviations above the mean}$$

$$\left.\begin{array}{l} 29 - 32 = -3 \\ 28 - 32 = -4 \\ 27 - 32 = -5 \\ 20 - 32 = -12 \end{array}\right] -24 \quad \text{deviations below the mean}$$

Note: The sum of positive and negative values should always equal zero.

STEP 3 Square each deviation and find the mean of the squares.

$$\frac{(+21)^2 + (+3)^2 + (-3)^2 + (-4)^2 + (-5)^2 + (-12)^2}{6} = \frac{644}{6} = 107.3333$$

STEP 4 Find the standard deviation by taking the square root of the mean in Step 3.

$$\sqrt{107.3333} = 10.360\ldots \approx 10$$

A small standard deviation suggests that the values are spaced near the mean and a large standard deviation suggests a greater spread of values.

A *normal curve* is a bell shaped curve that closely matches the distribution of many large sets of numbers.

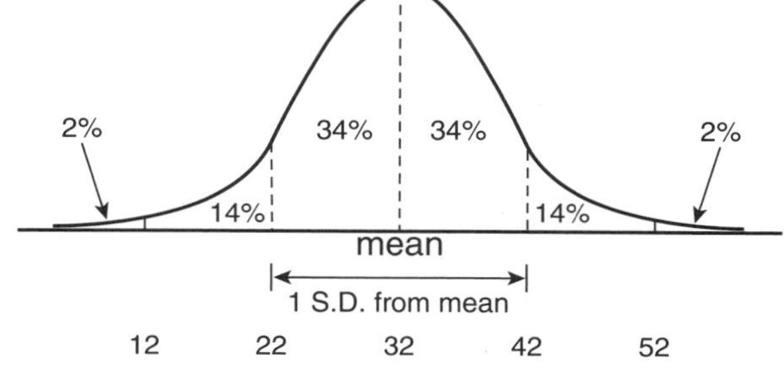

EXERCISE 11.0

For each of the following problems, find (a) the mean, (b) the median, (c) the mode, (d) the range, and (e) the standard deviation to nearest whole number.

1. 25, 52, 48, 58, 52, 38, 42

2. 75, 83, 93, 65, 85, 88, 90, 85, 71, 55

3. Annual income of eight families

$35,000, $70,000, $15,000, $20,000, $18,000, $12,000, $15,000, $17,000

4. The Smith's monthly electric bills for 1995 are:

$103.64	$102.74	$69.41	$95.95
96.96	101.08	77.95	101.72
100.60	100.50	92.18	104.72

POST TEST

The following test is designed to help you assess your understanding of the basics, applications, and graphs presented in this book. There is no time limit in taking the post test. Answers to the test questions are given near the end of the book.

PART I

1. Indicate the place value of each digit in 7,903.

2. Write the number 16,123 in words.

3. 55 + 33 + 16 + 12 = ?

4. Find the sum:

$$\begin{array}{r} 16{,}302 \\ 1{,}711 \\ 548 \\ 13 \\ +\ 7{,}502 \\ \hline \end{array}$$

5. If a minuend is 4,781 and the subtrahend is 439, what is the difference?

6. The balance in Samantha's checkbook is $933. If she writes a check for $13.42 and another check for $119.37, what is her new balance?

7. 47,301 − 29,487 = ?

8. 1,836 × 47 = ?

9. Joey bought nine tickets in a church raffle and paid $4.00 per ticket. How much did she pay?

10. If a case of motor oil contains 32 cans, how many cans of oil would there be in 159 cases?

11. 29,533 ÷ 7= ?

12. What is the average height in inches of five children whose heights are 42 inches, 54 inches, 47 inches, 39 inches, and 53 inches?

$$\left(\text{Average height} = \frac{\text{Sum of heights}}{\text{Number of children}}\right)$$

13. How much is your weekly pay if your yearly salary is $40,872?

14. Write $\frac{14}{46}$ in lowest terms.

15. Convert $5\frac{7}{9}$ to an improper fraction.

16. Convert the improper fraction $\frac{41}{3}$ to a mixed number.

17. What is the sum of $\frac{11}{31} + \frac{15}{31} + \frac{2}{31}$?

18. $\frac{3}{5} + \frac{2}{7} + \frac{1}{3} = ?$

19. $\frac{11}{13} - \frac{2}{3} = ?$

20. $8\frac{1}{6} - 2\frac{3}{4} = ?$

21. $14 - \left(1\frac{7}{8} + 3\frac{1}{4}\right) = ?$

22. $\frac{4}{9} \times \frac{1}{12} = ?$

23. $2\frac{2}{3} \times 6\frac{3}{5} = ?$

24. $\frac{3}{5} \div \frac{12}{25} = ?$

25. $22 \div 3\frac{1}{3} = ?$

26. Write the number 17.23 in words.

POST TEST (continued)

27. Convert 0.102 to an equivalent common fraction in lowest terms.

28. Convert $\frac{5}{12}$ to its decimal equivalent, correct to the nearest ten-thousandth.

29. $3.15 + $21.03 + $7.99 = ?

30. The temperature at 1 p.m. was 87.3°. At 8 p.m. it was 64.5°. What was the drop in temperature?

31. If you bought 17 hammers at $7.35 each, how much money did you pay?

32. If you drove 872.7 miles on 19.8 gallons of gasoline, how many miles did you get per gallon of gasoline?

33. Convert 0.637 to a percentage.

34. Convert 31.01% to a decimal.

35. Convert $\frac{9}{5}$ to a percentage.

36. Convert 30.1% to a fraction.

PART II

37. Solve for x: $3x + 7 = 22$

38. Solve for y: $y + 1 = 3y - 5$

39. Solve for z: $2.3 = 0.4z - 21.1$

40. Solve for x: $4x = 2x + ab$

41. Solve for x: $\frac{a - b}{x} = 5a$

42. Given $I = PRT$. Find T if $P = \$9{,}000$, $R = 4.5\%$, and $I = \$810$.

43. Given $A = P(1 + RT)$. Find R if $P = \$14{,}600$, $T = 6$ months, and $A = \$15{,}745$.

PART III

44. What percentage of 300 is 18?

45. Twenty is 25% of what number?

46. What is $2\frac{1}{4}$% of 430?

47. If you receive a commission of 4.7% of net sales and your net sales totaled $7,532.54, what was your commission?

48. John sold products totaling $12,750 and received a commission of $669.38. What was his rate of commission?

49. What is the markup of a table saw that costs $450 and sells for $589.99? What is the rate of markup?

50. Each winter morning I turn my thermostat up from 60°F to 68°F. What is the percent increase in the thermostat reading?

51. If the original price of a snowblower has been discounted 35% to $610, what was the original price?

52. A retail store allows its employees a 12% discount on any purchase. How much would an employee pay on an item that normally cost $79.95?

53. A meal at the Gourmet Restaurant cost $34.87. If you had to pay a meal tax of $2\frac{1}{2}$% and you intended to leave a 20% tip, how much would you pay in total?

54. Determine the amount of property tax on property whose assessed value is $237,800 at a tax rate of $11.40 per $1,000.

55. What is the assessed value correct to the nearest dollar on a building if the property tax is $1,407.45 and the tax rate is 1.36%?

56. What is the amount of simple interest paid on a $6,540 loan for three months at 12%?

57. What would be the monthly payments in problem 56?

58. A 12-month installment loan with $35 payments and an interest charge of $50 was paid in full at the end of 9 months. How much was the final payment? (***HINT:*** Recall the Rule of 78ths)

POST TEST (continued)

PART IV

59. The manufacturing costs in producing a widget are as follows: research and development, $136,800; labor, $125,000; material costs, $180,500. Construct a circle graph showing this data.

Use the following graph to answer questions 60–63.

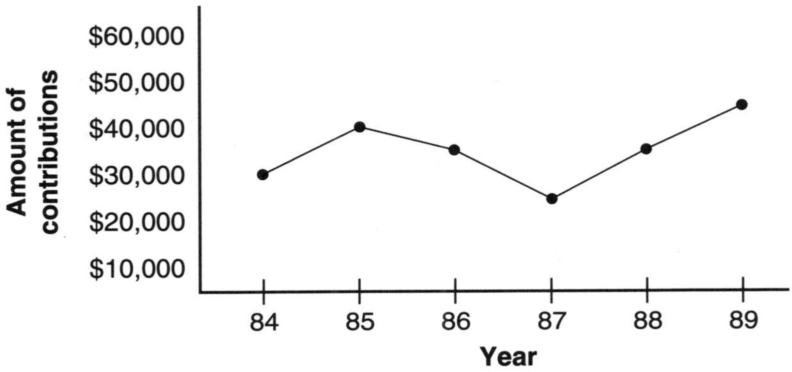

60. In which year were the fewest contributions made?

61. Between what years was there the greatest decrease in contributions?

62. What was the average yearly contribution during the six-year period?

63. Write a ratio comparing the contributions in 1986 to those in 1984.

64. What is the mean, median, mode, and range for the following temperatures?

    23°F, 37°F, 29°F, 54°F, 46°F, 37°F, 71°F, 67°F

65. Use unit fraction(s) to convert the following:

$$\frac{6 \text{ pints}}{\text{seconds}} = \frac{\text{gallons}}{\text{minute}}$$

66. Find the compound interest on an initial investment of $7,000 at 6% compounded semiannually for four years.

67. What fraction is represented the shaded portion of the figure below?

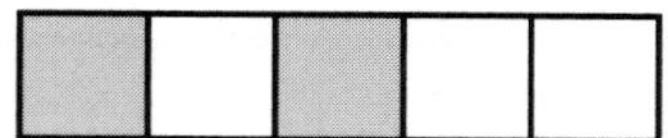

68. Given that 1 liter is approximately equal to 1.06 quarts, approximately how many liters to the nearest tenth are there in 12.4 quarts?

69. Find the standard deviation of this set of data:

4, 6, 8, 15, 17

EXERCISE ANSWERS

ANSWERS TO EXERCISE 1.1

1. 4, 3 9 1

4,	3	9	1
Thousands	Hundreds	Tens	Ones

2. 8, 4 7 3

8,	4	7	3
		Tens	

3. 11,362

4. 7,000,403

5. Three hundred forty-five thousand, six hundred seventy-eight

6. Nineteen thousand, one hundred ninety-one

7. 5, 0 1 2

5,	0	1	2
Thousands	Hundreds	Tens	Ones

8. Ten thousands

9. 117,347

10. One thousand, two hundred thirty-four

11. Four hundred three thousand, fifty-seven

12. 3,950

13. 3,900

14. 200,000

15. 8,000

ANSWERS TO EXERCISE 1.2

1. 120

2. 1,689

3. 131

4. $4,820

5. (a) Mon.: 26; Tues.: 29; Wed.: 30; Thurs.: 28; Fri.: 47; Sat.: 25
   (b) Brand K: 52; Brand P: 76; Brand G: 57
   (c) Total for the week: 185
6. 4,945
7. 4,070
8. $1,067
9. 95,713
10. $222
11. a) July: $13,006; August: $16,076; September: $23,172
    b) Maria: $3,478; Joe: $15,559; Mohammed: $20,852; Yoko: $12,365
    c) Total third-quarter commissions: $52,254
12. 10 pounds, 8 ounces, or $10^1/_2$ pounds

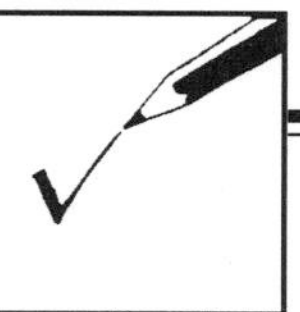

ANSWERS TO EXERCISE 1.3

1. 794
2. 7,755
3. 2 pounds, 14 ounces
4. (a) 13 minutes, 40 seconds; (b) 1 hour, 1 minute, 6 seconds
5. 2,172
6. 9,317
7. 118,113
8. $808
9. 2,253
10. $34,405
11. $1,525
12. 29 apartments

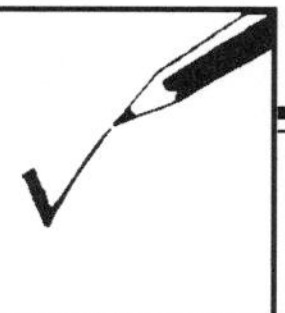

ANSWERS TO EXERCISE 1.4

1. 81,473
2. $4,875
3. 5,400
4. $192
5. $49,896
6. $3,910
7. $315
8. $2,280
9. 275 miles
10. 63 bushels
11. $496
12. 1,400 passengers

ANSWERS TO EXERCISE 1.5

1. 60
2. There is no quotient. You can't divide by zero.
3. $\frac{504}{6} = 84$
4. $\begin{array}{r}\$950\\ 800\overline{)\$760{,}000}\end{array}$ $\begin{array}{r}265\\ \$950\overline{)\$251{,}750}\end{array}$ 265 PCs
5. (a) 156; (b) 847
6. 605
7. $27
8. 8.2 calls per day; yes
9. $783
10. $808.53
11. 75.7, rounded to 76
12. mpg = 40.75, or approximately 41 mpg

ANSWERS TO EXERCISE 2.1

1. $\frac{3}{8}$
2.
3. $\frac{2}{7}$
4. $\frac{5}{6}$
5. $\frac{7}{4}$
6. $\frac{15}{26}$
7. $\frac{3}{11}$
8. $\frac{28}{17}$
9. $\frac{25}{33}$
10. $\frac{1}{3}$
11. $\frac{5}{16}$
12. 4 yards
13. 8 quarts
14. 256 ounces
15. 5 hours
16. 3 miles
17. $\frac{29}{4}$
18. $\frac{43}{7}$

19. $\frac{44}{9}$ **20.** $\frac{47}{11}$ **21.** $\frac{57}{8}$

22. $\frac{65}{7}$ **23.** $\frac{23}{8}$ **24.** $\frac{66}{13}$

25. $9\frac{4}{5}$ **26.** $33\frac{1}{3}$ **27.** $7\frac{3}{4}$

28. $2\frac{2}{3}$ **29.** $7\frac{4}{7}$ **30.** $9\frac{1}{6}$

31. $24\frac{3}{11}$ **32.** $39\frac{7}{11}$

ANSWERS TO EXERCISE 2.2

1. $\frac{3}{5}$ **2.** $\frac{4}{11}$ **3.** $\frac{12}{17}$

4. $1\frac{8}{19}$ **5.** $1\frac{3}{4}$ **6.** $2\frac{1}{7}$

7. $\frac{10}{5}$, or 2

ANSWERS TO EXERCISE 2.3

1. 40 **2.** 147 **3.** 108

ANSWERS TO EXERCISE 2.4

1. $\frac{1}{2}$	**2.** $\frac{26}{15}$, or $1\frac{11}{15}$	**3.** $\frac{227}{240}$
4. $2\frac{239}{315}$	**5.** $1\frac{3}{56}$	**6.** $\frac{27}{20}$, or $1\frac{7}{20}$
7. $\frac{18}{17}$, or $1\frac{1}{17}$	**8.** 2	**9.** $\frac{43}{36}$, or $1\frac{7}{36}$
10. $\frac{163}{63}$, or $2\frac{37}{63}$	**11.** $5\frac{5}{6}$	**12.** $15\frac{1}{3}$
13. $14\frac{1}{9}$	**14.** $5\frac{1}{10}$	**15.** $14\frac{1}{28}$
16. $10\frac{11}{60}$	**17.** $15\frac{1}{4}$ column inches	

ANSWERS TO EXERCISE 2.5

1. $\frac{6}{17}$	**2.** $\frac{14}{65}$	**3.** $\frac{25}{187}$
4. $\frac{2}{15}$	**5.** $\frac{5}{16}$	**6.** $\frac{1}{12}$
7. 0	**8.** $2\frac{13}{24}$	**9.** $38\frac{19}{42}$
10. $8\frac{11}{13}$	**11.** $6\frac{17}{60}$	**12.** $2\frac{7}{72}$

ANSWERS TO EXERCISE 2.6

1. $\frac{2}{35}$
2. $\frac{20}{117}$
3. $\frac{5}{6}$
4. $\frac{3}{20}$
5. $\frac{5}{12}$
6. $\frac{1}{9}$
7. $\frac{7}{26}$
8. $\frac{7}{4}$
9. 30
10. 68
11. $\frac{1}{2}$
12. $6\frac{19}{28}$
13. 0
14. $34\frac{2}{5}$
15. $\frac{100}{357}$
16. $\frac{93}{140}$
17. $\frac{11}{189}$
18. $\frac{3}{10}$
19. 2 cups corn kernels $\frac{2}{1} \times \frac{9}{4} = \frac{9}{2}$ or $4\frac{1}{2}$

    4 eggs $\frac{4}{1} \times \frac{9}{4} = 9$

    1 cup cream $\frac{1}{1} \times \frac{9}{4} = \frac{9}{4}$ or $2\frac{1}{4}$

    1 tablespoon sugar $\frac{1}{1} \times \frac{9}{4} = 2\frac{1}{4}$

    1 teaspoon salt $\frac{1}{1} \times \frac{9}{4} = 2\frac{1}{4}$

    $\frac{1}{4}$ teaspoon ground white pepper $\frac{1}{4} \times \frac{9}{4} = \frac{9}{16}$

    Dash nutmeg + 2 tablespoon butter $\frac{2}{1} \times \frac{9}{4} = 4\frac{1}{2}$

ANSWERS TO EXERCISE 2.7

1. $\frac{4}{3}$, or $1\frac{1}{3}$
2. $\frac{9}{50}$
3. 0
4. Impossible; can't divide by zero.
5. $\frac{9}{14}$
6. $\frac{5}{4}$, or $1\frac{1}{4}$
7. $\frac{32}{3}$, or $10\frac{2}{3}$
8. $\frac{3}{32}$
9. $\frac{3}{22}$
10. $\frac{207}{703}$
11. $59\frac{37}{81}$

ANSWERS TO EXERCISE 3.1

1. 0.80
2. 8.75
3. 0.01
4. 0.87
5. 72.44
6. 0.56
7. 0.33
8. 0.25
9. 0.90
10. 0.78
11. 0.20
12. 0.78

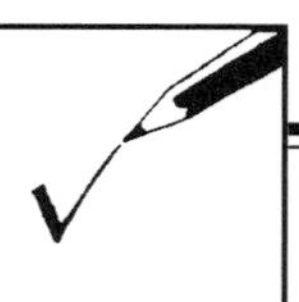

ANSWERS TO EXERCISE 3.2

1. $\frac{1}{500}$
2. $\frac{33}{20}$
3. $\frac{9}{100}$
4. $\frac{17}{100}$
5. $\frac{123}{1,000}$
6. $\frac{23}{10}$

7. $\frac{853}{50}$ **8.** $\frac{37}{10{,}000}$ **9.** $\frac{13{,}013}{50}$

10. $\frac{871}{1{,}000}$ **11.** $\frac{15}{4}$ **12.** $\frac{2{,}006}{10{,}000}$, or $\frac{1{,}003}{5{,}000}$

ANSWERS TO EXERCISE 3.3

1. 259.974 **2.** $699.96 **3.** $2,302.93
4. 68.646 **5.** 51.7106 **6.** $2,554.39
7. $2,324.17 **8.** 531.8 miles
9. 7.52 km (approximately 4.7 miles)

ANSWERS TO EXERCISE 3.4

1. 4.25 **2.** 35.497 **3.** 439.421
4. 4.1° **5.** $15.66 **6.** 14.86467
7. $18.67 **8.** $357.45 **9.** 1:53 P.M.

ANSWERS TO EXERCISE 3.5

1. 3.5 **2.** 0.010 **3.** 14.567987
4. 5.01 **5.** 2.01 **6.** 1.85
7. 14.0 **8.** 0.2469

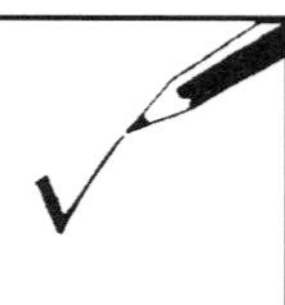

ANSWERS TO EXERCISE 3.6

1. 2,317
2. 334.03368
3. $13.95
4. $1,325.34
5. 0.013284
6. $217,050
7. 197 miles
8. $4.74
9. $1,240.80
10. $403.75
11. $7,845.30
12. (a) 1,750 mL; (b) 330 mL; (c) 2,369.4 mL
13. $1,395 shipping chargey

ANSWERS TO EXERCISE 3.7

1. 6.28
2. 0.01
3. 1,224.80
4. $64,785.71
5. 0.03
6. 0.01
7. (a) 15 L; (b) 0.00135 L; (c) 0.860 L
8. $768.45 U.S.
9. (a) BMI = 25; (b) BMI = 41+
10. $1,796.69
11. 133.38 gal.
12. $2,350 per square foot
13. 237.40 gal.
14. A 60-foot hose costing $10.49

ANSWERS TO EXERCISE 4.0

1. 11,105%
2. 0.45%
3. 3%
4. 31%
5. 5.54%
6. 12,500%
7. 9,320%
8. 4567%
9. 2%
10. 99%
11. (a) 20 kg; (b) 90 kg
12. 75%

13. $\frac{5}{8} = 0.625$, or 62.5%
14. 0.93
15. 0.000025
16. 0.83
17. 1.5
18. 0.164
19. 0.0045
20. 1.01
21. 180%
22. 53.7%
23. $\frac{1{,}633}{2{,}000}$
24. $\frac{4{,}001}{1{,}000}$, or $4\frac{1}{1{,}000}$
25. $\frac{1}{6}$
26. $\frac{1}{9}$
27. $\frac{13}{150}$
28. $\frac{1}{800}$
29. $2\frac{1}{20}$

ANSWERS TO EXERCISE 5.0

1. $y = 2$
2. $x = 636$
3. $x = 12$
4. $x = 60.25$
5. $x = 3$
6. $p = 7$
7. $w = 15$
8. $z = 52.9$
9. $y = \frac{3}{5}$
10. $m = 5\frac{3}{4}$
11. $x = \frac{27}{40}$
12. $x = \frac{23}{28}$
13. $y = \frac{8}{5}$, or $1\frac{3}{5}$
14. $x = \frac{15}{2}$, or $7\frac{1}{2}$
15. $z = 0.2$
16. $x = 0.0028$
17. $y = 38.8$
18. $x = \frac{4}{7}$

ANSWERS TO EXERCISE 6.0

1. $2x + y = 6$
   $y = 6 - 2x$

2. $D = RT$
   $D = (55 \text{ mph})(3.5 \text{ hr.}) = 192.5 \text{ mi.}$

3. $P = \dfrac{L + I}{T}$

   $P = \dfrac{\$800 + 800(2)(.124)}{2} = \dfrac{800 + 198.4}{2} = \dfrac{998.4}{2} = \$499.20$

4. $T = \dfrac{I}{PR}$

5. $h = \dfrac{2A}{b}$

6. $P = EY - Y$

7. $m = \dfrac{y - b}{xt}$

8. $V_2 = \dfrac{V_1T_2}{T_1}$

9. $810

10. $11,900

11. 5

12. $15,074.50

ANSWERS TO EXERCISE 7.1

1. $P = RB$
   $49 = R(102)$
   $R = \dfrac{49}{102} = 48.04\%$

2. $16 = .80B$
   $B = \dfrac{16}{.80} = 20$

3. $P = 0.0106(500) = 5.3$

4. 3.75

5. 13

6. 55.775

7. 30432.2746

8. 2.5%

9. 38.4

10. 13.50

11. 2,000

12. $12,857

13. (a) 102 to 134 beats/minute; (b) 132 to 173 beats/minute

ANSWERS TO EXERCISE 7.2

1. $C = \$53{,}720 \times 11\% = \$5{,}909.20$
2. $\$3{,}670.40 = R \times \$47{,}533;\ R = 7.6\%$
3. $5,957.45
4. $705.06
5. $363.76
6. $240.72
7. $2,794
8. $34,991.11
9. $946.44

ANSWERS TO EXERCISE 7.3

1. $12\frac{1}{2}\%$
2. 9.6%
3. 7.7%
4. 7.2%
5. (a) $41.73; (b) 35%
6. $207.50
7. $108
8. $33\frac{1}{3}\%$
9. 39%
10. $320.60
11. $19,152

ANSWERS TO EXERCISE 7.4

1. $736 – $573.45 = $162.55, the amount of decrease

$$R = \frac{\$162.55}{\$736} = 22\%, \text{ or } 0.22$$

2. Amount of decrease = 192 lb. – 179 lb. = 13 lb.

$$R = \frac{13 \text{ lb.}}{192 \text{ lb.}} = .0677, \text{ or } 7\%$$

3. $13.50 − $11.85 = $1.65

$$R = \frac{P}{B} = \frac{\$1.65}{\$13.50} = 0.12, \text{ or } 12\%$$

4. 9.50%
5. (a) $80; (b) $64
6. $950
7. (a) Break-even point is $324.58; (b) profit of $20.37
8. 67,000

ANSWERS TO EXERCISE 7.5

1. $R = \dfrac{\$75}{\$600} = 0.125, \text{ or } 12.5\%$

2. Discount = 0.15 × $1,525 = $228.75

   Sale price = Marked price − Discount
   = $1,525 − $228.75 = $1,296.25

3. Discount = 0.03 × $537.38 = $16.12

   Discounted payment = $537.38 − $16.12 = $521.26

4. 4 × $86 = $344

   Discount = $344 × 0.20 = $68.80

   Total price = $344 − $68.80 = $275.20

5. Discount = Rate of discount × Regular price

   $95 = 0.55 × Regular price

   $$\text{Regular price} = \frac{\$95}{0.55} = \$172.73$$

ANSWERS TO EXERCISE 7.6

1. Sales tax = 0.025 × $120 = $3
2. $549 × 0.06 = $32.94 (state sales tax)
   $549 × 0.015 = $8.24 (city sales tax)
   $549 + $32.94 + $8.24 = $590.18 (total cost)
3. $195 × 0.05 = $9.75 (discount)
   $195 – $9.75 = $185.25 (sales price)
   $185 × 0.035 = $6.48 (sales tax)
   $185.25 + $6.48 = $191.73 (total cost)
4. $\text{Sales tax rate} = \dfrac{\text{Sales tax}}{\text{Purchse price}} = \dfrac{\$14.20}{\$495} = 0.0286, \text{ or } 2.9\%$
5. $53.19
6. 3.5%
7. $129.55
8. $3,641.18
9. 4%

ANSWERS TO EXERCISE 7.7

1. $\dfrac{\$760,000}{\$1,000} = 760$
   $760 \times \$12.50 = \$9,500$
2. $\dfrac{\$34,500}{\$1,000} = 34.5$
   $34.5 \times \$16.50 = \$569.25$
3. $2,513.28
4. 4.67%
5. $2,845.38
6. $103,489
7. $5,907.06
8. $472.82

ANSWERS TO EXERCISE 7.8

1. $I = PRT = (\$550)(0.08)(\frac{1}{2}) = \$22$
2. There are 80 days between the dates.

   $I = (\$450)(0.0975)\left(\frac{80}{360}\right) = \$9.75$

3. 9%
4. $1,181.25
5. $423.73
6. February 12, 1991
7. $6.75
8. $51.25
9. $3,428.48 (amount); $428.48 (interest)
10. $900
11. $162.96
12. $3,642.23

ANSWERS TO EXERCISE 7.9

1. $\$50 + (\$60 \times 18) = \$1,130$
   $\$1,130 - \$1,000 = \$130$
2. $\$1,450 - \$250 = \$1,200$, the amount financed
   $\$1,200(0.105)(\frac{9}{12}) = \$94.50$, the finance charge
   $\$1,200 + \$94.50 = \$1,294.50$, the total installment payment
   $\$1,294.50 \div 9 = \$143.83$, the monthly payment
3. $0
4. $\$275 \times 0.012 = \$3.30$
   $\$275 + \$3.30 = \$278.30$
5. $60.00
6. $9,375
7. (a) $2,8982.81; (b) $15,382.81
8. (a) $1,785; (b) $912.50; (c) $51,252.50
9. $\frac{21}{78}$
10. $660.84

ANSWERS TO EXERCISE 8.0

1. 1985
2. 1980
3. 200%
4. $425
5. **Troy Clothiers Sales, January through June**

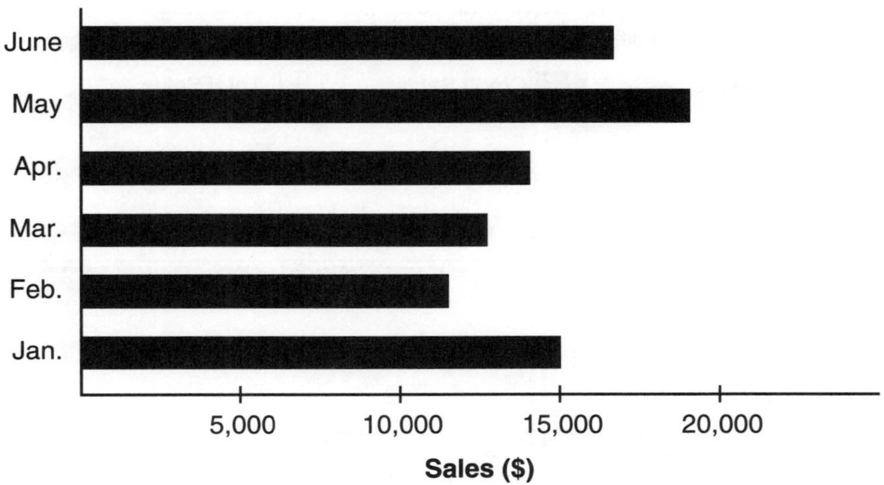

6. **Big Mike's Sales, 1985–1989**

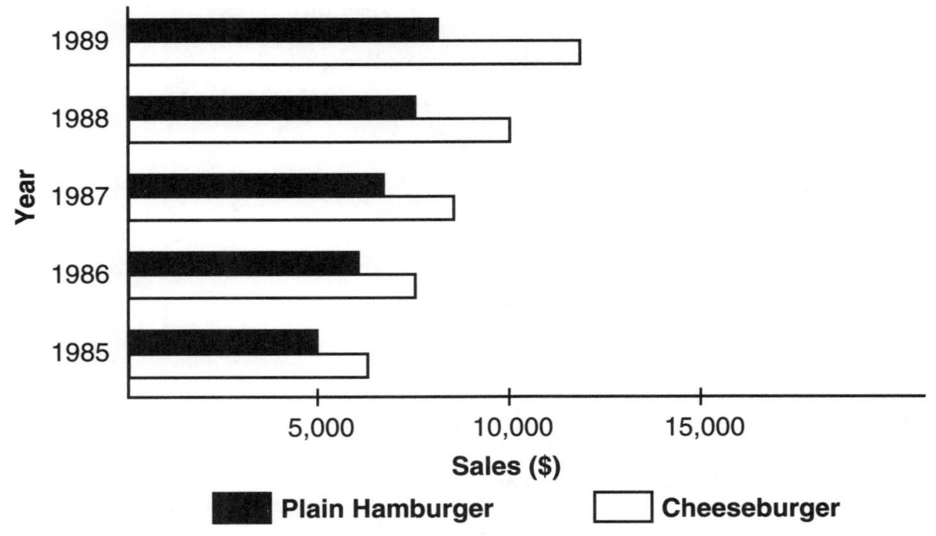

7.

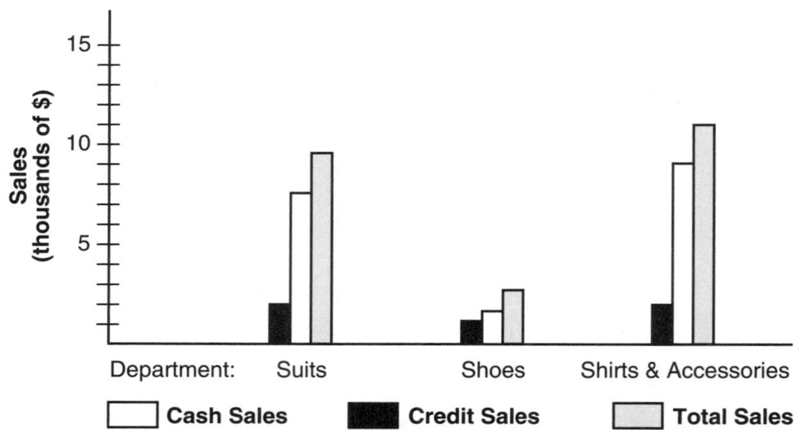

8. $\frac{20}{50}$, or $\frac{2}{5}$

9. Between 1970 and 1980

10. An increase

ANSWERS TO EXERCISE 9.0

1. 1972
2. 22.2%
3. 50 million
4. 12.5%
5.

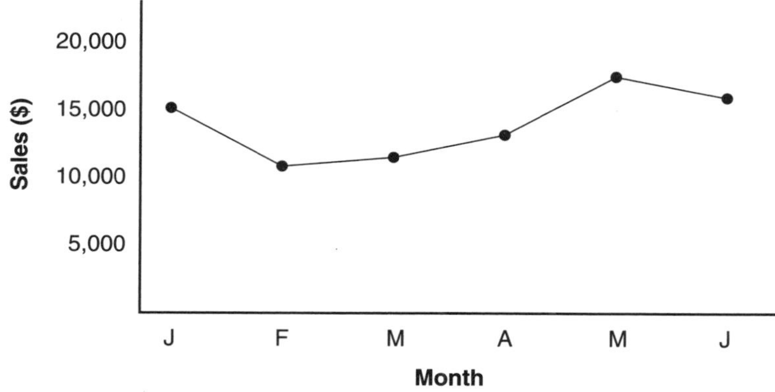

ANSWERS TO EXERCISE 10.0

1. $8,400
2. $48,000
3. 100%
4. **Pennyroyal Herb Farm Revenues**

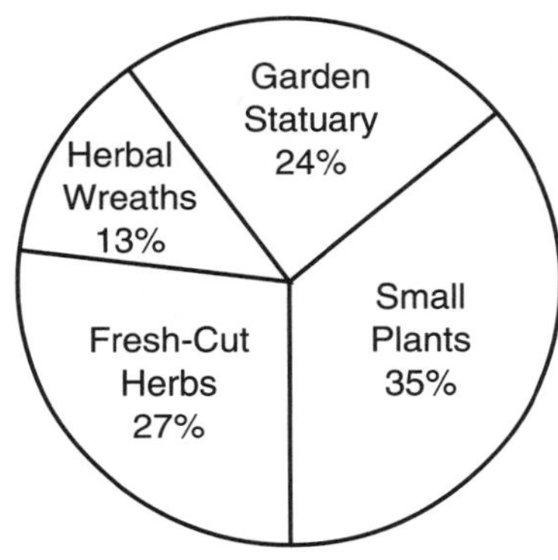

5. **New Paul College: A, B, and C Students**

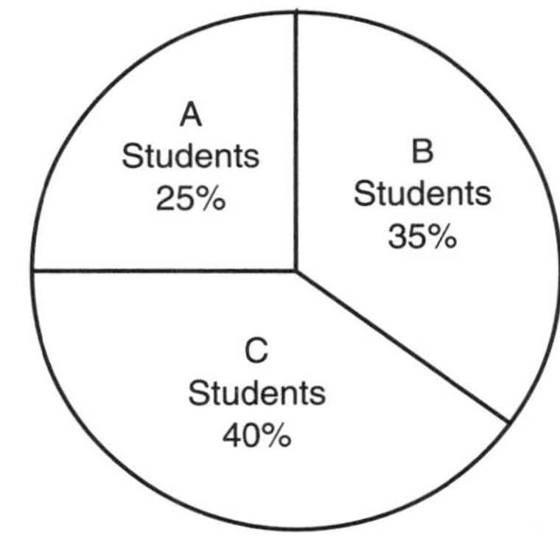

EXERCISE 11.0 ANSWERS

1. 45, mean; 48, median; 52, mode; 33, range; 10, standard deviation
2. 79, mean; 84, median; 85, mode; 38, range; 12, standard deviation
3. $25,250, mean; $17,500, median; $15,000, mode; $58,000, range; $18,137, standard deviation
4. $95.62, mean; $100.55, median; none, mode; $35.31, range; $11, standard deviation

POST TEST ANSWERS

PART I

1. 7, 9 0 3 — 7 Thousands, 9 Hundreds, 0 Tens, 3 Ones

2. Sixteen thousand, one hundred twenty-three

3. 116
4. 26,076
5. 4,342 is the difference
6. $800.21
7. 17,814
8. 86,292
9. $36
10. 5,088 cans
11. 4,219
12. 47 inches
13. $786
14. $\frac{7}{23}$
15. $\frac{52}{9}$
16. $13\frac{2}{3}$
17. $\frac{28}{31}$
18. $\frac{128}{105}$, or $1\frac{23}{105}$
19. $\frac{7}{39}$
20. $\frac{65}{12}$, or $5\frac{5}{12}$
21. $\frac{71}{8}$, or $8\frac{7}{8}$
22. $\frac{1}{27}$
23. $\frac{88}{5}$, or $17\frac{3}{5}$
24. $\frac{5}{4}$
25. $6\frac{2}{3}$
26. Seventeen and twenty-three hundredths
27. $\frac{51}{500}$
28. 0.4167
29. $32.17
30. 22.8°
31. $124.95
32. Approximately 44.1 miles per gallon
33. 63.7%
34. 0.3101
35. 180%
36. $\frac{301}{1,000}$

PART II

37. $x = 5$
38. $y = 3$
39. $z = 58.5$

40. $x = \frac{ab}{2}$

41. $x = \frac{a - b}{5a}$

42. $T = 2$

43. 15.7%

PART III

44. 6%

45. 80

46. 9.675

47. $354.03

48. $5\frac{1}{4}\%$

49. $139.99; 31.1%

50. 13.3%

51. $938.46

52. $70.36

53. $42.71

54. $2,710.92

55. $103,489

56. $196.20

57. $2,245.40

58. $101.15

PART IV

59. **Manufacturing Costs**

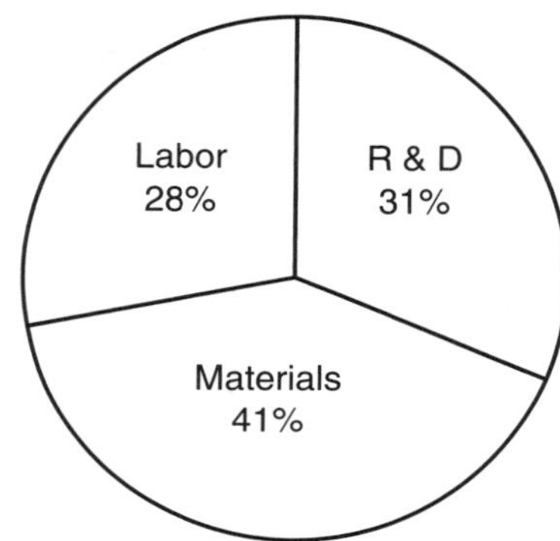

60. 1987

61. Between 1986 and 1987

62. $37,000

63. $\frac{358}{30}$, or $\frac{7}{6}$

64. Mean = 45.5°; median = 41.5°; mode = 37°; range = 48°

65. $\frac{\text{45 gallons}}{\text{minute}}$

66. $8,867.39

67. $\frac{2}{5}$

68. 11.7

69. 11

GLOSSARY
THE LANGUAGE OF ALGEBRA

	Word Expression	Algebraic Expression
Addition:	Add; added to; the sum of; more than; increased by; the total of; plus	$+$
	Add x and y	$x + y$
	y added to 7	$7 + y$
	The sum of a and b	$a + b$
	m more than n	$n + m$
	p increased by 10	$p + 10$
	The total of q and 10	$q + 10$
	9 plus m	$9 + m$
Subtraction:	Subtract; subtract from; difference between; less; less than; decreased by; diminished by; take away; reduced by; exceeds; minus	$-$
	Subtract x from y	$y - x$
	From x, subtract y	$x - y$
	The difference between x and 7	$x - 7$
	10 less m	$10 - m$
	10 less than m	$m - 10$
	p decreased by 11	$p - 11$
	8 diminished by w	$8 - w$
	y take away z	$y - z$
	p reduced by 6	$p - 6$
	x exceeds y	$x - y$
	r minus s	$r - s$
Multiplication:	Multiply; times; the product of; multiplied by; times as much; of	$\times$
	Multiply x and y	xy
	7 times y	$7y$
	The product of x and y	xy
	5 multiplied by y	$5y$
	$\frac{1}{5}$ of p	$\frac{1}{5}p$

GLOSSARY (continued)

	Word Expression	Algebraic Expression
Division:	Divide; divides; divided by; the quotient of; the ratio of; equal amounts of; per	$\div$
	Divide x by 6	$\frac{x}{6}$ or $x \div 6$
	7 divides x	$\frac{x}{7}$ or $x \div 7$
	7 divided by x	$\frac{7}{x}$ or $7 \div x$
	The quotient of y and 5	$\frac{y}{5}$ or $y \div 5$
	The ratio of u to v	$\frac{u}{v}$ or $u \div v$
	u separated into four equal parts	$\frac{u}{4}$ or $u \div 4$
	5 parts per 100 parts	$\frac{5}{100}$
Power:	The square of y	y^2
	The cube of k	k^3
	t raised to the fourth power	t^4
Equals:	Is equal to; the same as; is; are; the result of; will be; was	$=$
	x is equal to y	$x = y$
	p is the same as q	$p = q$
Multiplication by two:	Two, two times; twice; twice as much as; double	2
	Twice z	$2z$
	y doubled	$2y$
Multiplication by one-half:	Half of; one-half of; half as much as; one-half times	$\frac{1}{2}$
	Half of u	$\frac{1}{2}u$
	One-half times m	$\frac{1}{2}m$

THE METRIC SYSTEM

I. The basic units are *meter* (length), *liter* (capacity), and *gram* (weight).

Prefix	*Symbol*	*Meaning*
milli	m	one-thousandth of the basic unit
centi	c	one-hundredth of the basic unit
deci	d	one-tenth of the basic unit
deka	dk	ten times basic unit
hecto	h	one hundred times basic unit
kilo	k	one thousand times basic unit

Example:

gram	liter	meter
1 mg = 0.001 g	1 mL = 0.001 L	1 mm = 0.001 m
1 cg = 0.01 g	1 cL = 0.01 L	1 cm = 0.01 m
1 dg = 0.1 g	1 dL = 0.1 L	1 dm = 0.1 m
1 g = 1 g	1 L = 1 L	1 m = 1 m
1 dkg = 10 g	1 dkL = 10 L	1 dkm = 10 m
1 hg = 100 g	1 hL = 100 L	1 hm = 100 m
1 kg = 1000 g	1 kL = 1000 L	1 km = 1000 m

II. When changing to smaller metric units multiply by 10.

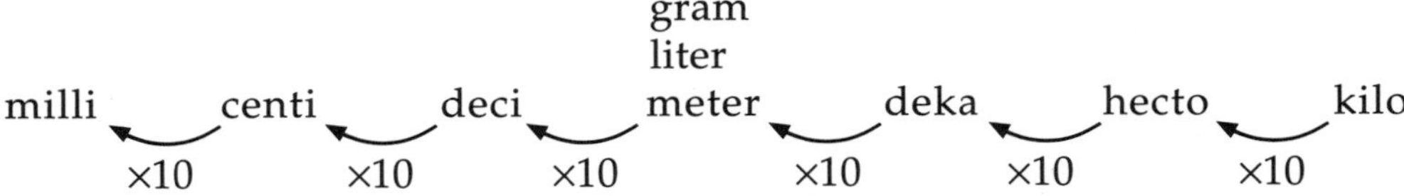

Example: 3.5 dkL = 35 L

THE METRIC SYSTEM (continued)

III. Changing to larger metric units divide by 10.

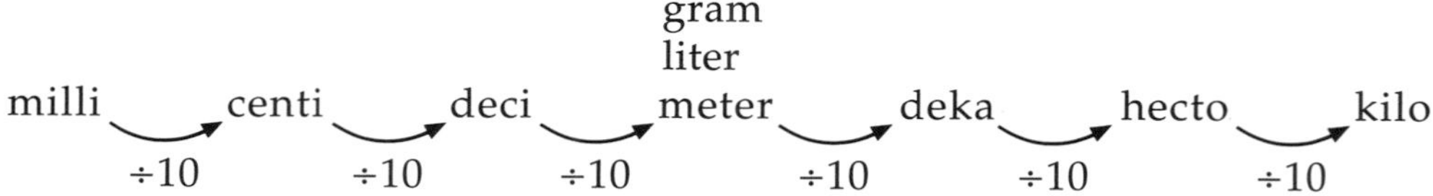

Example: 251 cm = 0.0251 hm

IV. Metric equivalents

a. English to metric

1 inch = 2.54 cm
1 inch = 0.0254 m
1 foot = 0.305 m
1 mile = 1.61 km
1 liquid quart = 0.95 L
1 dry quart = 1.1 L
1 ounce = 28.35 g
1 pound = 0.45 kg

b. Metric to English

1 cm = 0.39 inch
1 m = 39.37 inch
1 m = 3.28 foot
1 km = 0.62 mile
1 L = 1.06 liquid quarts
1 L = 0.91 dry quart
1 g = 0.04 ounce
1 kg = 2.2 pounds

Example:

a) 14 m = ? ft.

$$\frac{14\text{ m}}{1} \times \frac{\quad}{1\text{ m}} = 46.92\text{ ft}$$

b) 3 in = ? cm

$$\frac{3\text{ in}}{1} \times \frac{2.54\text{ cm}}{1\text{ in}} = 7.62\text{ cm}$$

NOTES

NOTES

NOTES

NOTES

NOTES

NOTES